I0117596

ALL RIGHTS RESERVED
PRINTED IN THE UNITED STATES OF AMERICA
First Edition: Ishai Publishers, December 1999

ISBN-10: 1892096056 ISBN-13: 978-1892096050
Second Edition: Effusses Enterprise: August 2009
ISBN: 978-0-578-03579-6

When The Children Get Together

A Novel By R. Bryant Smith

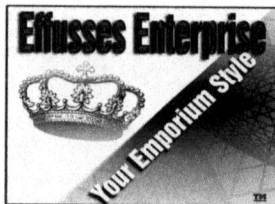

Effusses Enterprise

Austin, Texas

Preface

It is interesting how ten years can pass by so quickly, yet, ten years has passed by since the original printing of *When The Children Get Together*. What a journey this book has taken me on!

When it was first published, like all writers, I wanted to share the contents with everyone I knew especially my friends and loved ones from Dyer County. I quickly recognized that was truly a mistake in some senses yet a legendary landmark in others. Whereas I was under the assumption that the people who were dear to my heart were avid readers who read for comprehension, I discovered a miserable truth... most were not.

Since then, I still have people who dearly wanted me to chronicle their existence, come to me with the expression: "Oh, I heard that you included me in your first book." Hence, I immediately recognized that they never read my book or any of my work for if they had, they would have immediately recognized that my first novel chronicled nothing more than a view point as all written literature does. It was unfortunate, however, that these same people could not share in the mile stone victories that the rural South made during the season of Renaissance writing within African American Gay Literature. Instead, they had to hold fast to some idea that I had exposed them for who they truly are when in fact, no one really cares.

The journey has truly been a liberating journey as after the first publication of *When The Children Get Together* I actually learned how to let go of a past that has indeed passed me by. The Dyer County that I wrote about in the first novel ceases to exist because the world continued to change as did that precious Bruce Community that I shared with the world once upon a time. The community in which I wrote about had gone out of existence around the same time that the book was published. Those individuals who made African American society worthwhile had begun to die at alarming rates yet they forgot to pass the torch. In forgetting to pass the torch, the Dyer County that I remembered as being nostalgic; full of love; and a place to hang ones heart, vanished completely and can only be found in certain select cemeteries.

It is my hope and prayer, however, that all of those values are not completely forgotten and that the ugly hands of drugs and disease did not completely destroy a total way of life. However, I am sensible enough to realize that every civilization adapts or perishes. With that knowledge, I understand how my precious and nostalgic Dyer County evolved and adapted into a place where I am now the stranger to a completely dead way of life yet never a stranger to many of the wonderful memories that I obtained while growing up there.

Once again, *When the Children Get Together* is a story seen through the eyes of an African American young man who grew up in the rural south. His adventures are expressed from his own point of view.

Dedication

On all of the pages of my life, Granny, you have been there! I thank and praise God for the years He allowed you to be in my life! You have been the inspiring force for many of my accomplishments in life. I thank you for your watchful spirit that forever surrounds my well being and me. I shall meet you in Heaven one day… until then, thank you and I love you!

In Tribute to

Mrs. Barbara Ellen Chaney

Mr. Roy Bedford Smith, Junior

Mrs. Marilynn Perry Smith

My three amigos: My mother, my father, and my step-mother. All three are unique yet are a wealth of love, knowledge, compassion, and understanding. Thank you all for the roles that you play in my life and always know that I love you.

In Memoriam

"Gone But Not Forgotten"

We know that if our earthly house of this tabernacle were dissolved,
We have a building of God, a house not made with hands,
Eternal in the heavens.

2 Corinthians 5:1

Mr. Terry Townsend
November 10, 1964 – November 26, 1991

Mr. Terry Lee White
July 16, 1964 – February 18, 1992

Mr. Brandon Keith Kincaid
December 13, 1970 – October 19, 1992

Mr. Anthony "Surp" McDowell
February 8. 1954 – September 9, 1993

Mr. Joe N. Rice
March 14, 1965 – March 4, 1994

Mr. Riley Stefan "Bay-Bay" Thomas
May 5, 1962 – May 29, 1994

Mr. James "Smokey" Schaeffer, Junior
October 13, 1953 – March 27, 1995

Mr. Terry Dwayne Lyons
September 9, 1972 – June 5, 1997

Ms. Elaine Swift
June 10, 1972 – February 28, 1998

Mr. Tommy L. Swift, Junior
September 9, 1972 – February 28, 1999

Mr. Joseph Collins, IV
January 31, 1968 – March 5, 1999

Professor Johnny Lee Moore
July 23, 1947 – May 15, 1999

Mr. Diamond Demco Stewart
April 10, 1977 – January 29, 2001

Mr. Joel M Scott
June 10, 1970 – October 31, 2001

Mr. Sean J. Stafford
February 16, 1969 – May 23, 2002

Mr. Anthony O'Neil Dilworth
March 21, 1963 – May 2, 2003

Mr. Reginald Wooten

September 22, 1960 – August 25, 2006

Rev. Ernest Wayne Hammick

June 10, 1978 – September 15, 2006

Cortez Stewart

August 24, 1965 – July 15, 2009

Acknowledgements

*Just in case the Lord shall come before we get together again,
I'll meet you! Yes, I'll meet you on the other shore!*

A special thank you to the following people who continuously go the extra mile in making certain that I continue to write and I continue to be me.

All praises to God for His awesome wonder!

A special "Thanks" with endearing appreciation is extended to my parents: Ms Barbara Ellen Chaney, Mr. Roy B. Smith, Jr. and Mrs. Marilynn P. Smith. Truly you are the world's greatest parents.

I send "shout outs" to: Ms. CasSandra D.S. Anderson, Ms. Crystal D. Hickerson, and Ms. LeKeisha Weathers for being the world's greatest sisters.

I send "shout outs" to: Mr. Ryan B. Smith, Mr. RaShad B. Smith, Mr. Russell B. Smith, and Mr. Clayton P. Smith for being the world's greatest brothers.

A special "Thank You" is further extended to my dearest friends: Mr. DeAnthony J. Banks, Mr. Andrew Bradford, Mr. Marvin Hooper, Dr. & Atty. Carlos & Kerri Thomas, Prof. Bryan Keith Thomas, Dr. Victor Anderson, Rev. Harold K. Gause, Mrs. Patsy A. Coleman, Mrs. Patricia T. White, Ms. Stephanie Harris, Ms. Stephanie Watkins Pitts, Mr. Bryant Tyus, and Mr. Maurice Jones for being the best friends anyone could ever ask for.

How wonderful it is to have a collection of other artists who encourage you. I extend warm "thanks" to Rev. J. Ricc Rollins, Mr. Lorenzo Robertson, Mr. Darios Omar Williams, Mr. Greg McNeal, Mr. Timothy Hampton, and Mr. James Earl Hardy who are also friends who constantly encourage me along this journey of writ.

Last, a special "Thank You" is extended to other friends that I have met along the way.

May His peace be with you until we meet again!

When The Children Get Together

A Novel by R. Bryant Smith

Prologue

When all God's children get together,
What a time!

What a time!

What a time!

We're gonna sit down by the banks of the river

What a time1

What a time!

What a time!

A rainy afternoon found Melvin sitting on the front porch of his newly renovated three bedroom home drinking a tall glass of iced tea... reflecting! He had just received the news that there would be no choir rehearsal on that evening due to the rain. What a marvelous idea it was for people who had families to come home after work, unlike him. Nevertheless, it was perfect for Melvin. He had grown tired of the same old tired rehearsals, in the same old tired church, in the same old tired community, in the same old tired town. He often wondered why he put himself through the torture of trying to modernize a church that wanted to hold so begrudgingly to the past. For almost two decades, he had been a member of at least one of the church choirs at Mt. Carmel Missionary Baptist Church. He led a dutiful life of a faithful member of the church, a faithful member of the choir, a faithful choir director, and a faithful lead male vocalist of the choir.

As Melvin sat on the porch, the rainwater began to slowly pour down the side of the house. Tears began to stream down his face as he watched the water drip off of the shingles and fall into the flowerbed. He began to think about just how miserable his life actually was. He was an African American man living within the confines of a rural southern community. This mere fact was enough to drive the average African American man out of his wits.

What elated more misery to Melvin's life was a deeper fact. He was gay, alone, and living within this community where there were no possible prospects within at least ten miles from where he lived.

As Melvin sipped his tea, allowing the cool liquid to slowly slide down his throat, inspiration began to flow through his body.

I am actually a very comfortable young man, he thought. *I own my own home, my own vehicle, and I have a fairly decent paying job... no, I actually have a career! I have no dependents. I am reasonably attractive. I have good health and I even have great strength. I have a social standing within this society. I have plenty of friends. Why should I be depressed on this wretchedly rainy day?*

Indeed Melvin was successful in his own right. He was only twenty-seven years old. He was the first African American teller in Fairhaven's one bank. He was a member of Fairhaven's oldest African American church, Mt. Carmel Missionary Baptist Church. He owned his own home. His maternal grandfather had died and willed it to him. His home was furnished with the latest furnishings available. He drove an emerald green 1997 Honda Accord. His wardrobe was always impeccably chosen from Goldsmith's, Peebles, and J.C. Pennys or sometimes he ordered clothes from Charles Wythe of London. Socially, he was considered one of the most loveable and eligible bachelors in Fairhaven. He was, by all counts, a member of Fairhaven's African American elite. Being born the grandson of the founder of a city's only black owned funeral home provided him this luxury. His family accepted him and loved him unconditionally and as he was. Subsequently, his family had never thought about questioning his sexuality nor had he ever exposed his preference to his family. He was considered the perfect child in the eyesight of his mother. Because she had deemed him such, he planned to hold on to this title dearly.

Melvin was one of four children born to Clarence and Etta James. He was the youngest child and only boy. The James Family was considered a "well-to-do" family in Fairhaven. Clarence was now the owner of the town's only African American funeral home. He had come from a long line of morticians and funeral directors. His father had owned James funeral home in Fairhaven prior to his ownership. His grandfather had also owned James Funeral home in Points Bluff, Mississippi. His uncles and aunts owned funeral homes all over the south. It totally disgusted Clarence that Melvin declared that he would not go into the industry. Because Melvin had broken family tradition, Clarence remained extremely hurt and agitated with Melvin for years. He felt that Melvin had snubbed his nose up to the very thing that had offered him a "better-than-average" life. Clarice, Melvin's oldest sister, followed in her father's footsteps and became a licensed embalmer and funeral director. Clarice efficiently ran James funeral home in Fairhaven whenever Clarence was out of town on business. Etta was an eighth grade English teacher at Newbern Junior High School. Unlike Clarence, she could care less what occupations her children chose, as long as they chose an occupation that they enjoyed.

Melvin was an attractive man. His attributes and features were a true blend of both of his parents. Like Clarence, Melvin was average height standing five foot seven inches with broad shoulders and a small waist line. He and Clarence shared well defined cheekbones, a large yet narrow nose, and a dimpled chin. Like Etta, Melvin had small features as well that included small hands and feet. His skin color, like Etta's, was a smooth caramel color. His eyes were almond shaped like his father's and his lips were thin like his mother's. Like his father, Melvin was stubborn. When either of the two of them made their minds up, no one except the Lord could change it. In the same token, Melvin possessed the calm nature of his mother that seemed almost serene in comparison to his father's.

Melvin had graduated Lane College of Jackson, Tennessee one year later than he originally had anticipated. During his senior year at Lane, his grandfather Jeremiah Hanks became ill. Melvin spent an entire year pampering Jeremiah. His works, however, were to no avail. Jeremiah died.

Jeremiah meant the world to Melvin! A simple, elderly man who loved nothing but fishing and the songs of Mahalia Jackson would be a perfect description of Jeremiah. This pretty much summed up his twilight years. Jeremiah had been an employee of Fairhaven's one factory since 1933. He retired in 1990 exactly one year after the death of his beloved wife, Bertha Jameson Hanks. For the next three years, Jeremiah did what he loved best... fishing and going to church. Melvin was the only grandchild that spent time with him after the death of his wife. It was no surprise to anyone that upon his death, he willed all of his worldly possessions to Melvin.

After Bertha's death, Jeremiah and Melvin had become inseparable. Melvin would drive to his home every Saturday morning and take him fishing; spend the entire day with him; take him home with the catch of the day; help to clean and cook the fish; and then go for a Saturday evening haircut. The next morning, Melvin would be at his door bright and early to pick him up for Sunday school and morning Worship at Mt. Carmel where he served as a deacon and Sunday School teacher.

Melvin did not care that his Gramps had willed him $125,000.00, a home, and a priceless collection of gospel records recorded in the 1930s, 1940s, and 1950s. He was more interested in the life of his hero. Gramps Jeremiah had always been his hero. As a child, Gramps Jeremiah would allow him to walk the half mile to the Coleman Factory every weekend. Before they arrived at the factory, they would stop by miller's grocery Store and buy a pound of rag bologna, crackers, and two RC colas. They would eat and then proceed on to the factory where the workers would always greet Melvin and their foreman. They would remain at the factory until around noon and then they would leave and go fishing.

Unfortunately, Jeremiah could not live without his precious and beloved Bertha and in 1993, exactly four years after her death, Jeremiah died of a weak and worn heart. With his dying, Melvin became an established young man in Fairhaven and it was without the money from the James funeral Home.

Melvin graduated Lane College in 1994 with a Bachelor of Science Degree in Business Administration. He returned to Fairhaven in an attempt to bring order to his life. He applied for a job at Fairhaven's Planter's & Merchants Bank and received a position as a bank teller. He knew that he was in "good ole boy" country and would have to endure the "good ole boy" mentality in order to survive. It was one thing to place your money into the bank but it was quite a different story when you handled the money of people who really did not trust you to be able to think much less count. But for some reason unknown to him, he felt that there was some great purpose for his life in Fairhaven, Tennessee, although he remained constantly bored to tears and depressed beyond reason daily.

When boredom began to tear him into small pieces, he simply jumped into his car and headed to Dyersburg, Jackson, Union City, or Memphis. If this did not work, we would call his friends who lived in or near one of the respective cities which would afford him some type of amusement during these perilous moments.

"Hello," the brassy voice answered the phone on the first ring.

"What's up?" Melvin asked.

"Nothing much," the voice changed into a deep and sexy monotone.

Melvin decided to play along with the voice for a minute before he would bust the person.

"You, baby," Melvin continued.

"Oh, really, do tell?"

"What color is your draws, bitch?"

"Melvin," the voiced roared in laughter. "You fucka! I thought you were some of my fierce trade! Hell, I thought you were somebody!"

"I am, honey, and don't you forget it!" Melvin laughed. "What are you up to, Bradley?"

"Shit, notta," Bradley replied. "Getting ready to go and get me something to eat."

"Where you headed?" Melvin asked hoping to be invited. Melvin really enjoyed Bradley's company. Bradley and Melvin had been the best of friends since Middle School. Bradley lived in RoEllen. He was the son of the infamous Smith-Kelly Clan from an area named Rock spring. This clan was a big tobacco and cotton farming family known for their insatiable parties. No one in the county could give parties quite like the Smith-Kelly Clan and no one in the county could hold liquor quite like these people could either. Although a very wild and wooly group of people, they were very compassionate and humble.

"Let's go to the Pizza Hut!"

"Who said I wanted to go?" Melvin asked.

"Do you want to meet me there or do you want to drive by here?"

"I'll meet you at your place…"

"Bet," Bradley said. "See you in fifteen minutes."

"Bet," Melvin said as he hung up the telephone and breathed a sigh of relief. Bradley had always had a way of cheering him up or at least getting him out of his funks. Melvin was happy that Bradley had never attracted him sexually because their friendship was like none other. Brad was indeed a powerfully attractive man. Unfortunately, he was just not what Melvin wanted or needed in a significant other.

Although they seemed to be the odd couple, they were truly best friends. Bradley was not nor never would be a suit and tie man on a daily basis while Melvin swore by his. Melvin was a professional and worked in a professional environment while Bradley worked in a factory in Dyersburg when he desired to work for extra cash. Consequently, because of his occupation, Bradley's chest rippled with natural muscles while Melvin scarcely had any. Bradley was tall. Melvin was short. Melvin was soft spoken while Bradley was loud and boisterous. The two were indeed the odd couple.

As Melvin drove to Bradley's trailer in RoEllen, he tried to figure out why the two of them had never attempted to date over the years. It seemed just like yesterday when they had both discovered one another's "cup of tea" and now they were as thick as thieves.

Chapter One

Leaning On the Everlasting Arms

Oh how sweet to walk in this pilgrim's way!
Leaning on the everlasting arms!
What have I to dread? What have I to fear?
Leaning on the everlasting arms!

Fairhaven, Tennessee was located in the southeastern division of Dyer County, Tennessee. The population of Fairhaven was 3,000. Of that 3,000 people 850 were African American. The nearest town of any size was RoEllen, Trimble, or perhaps Newbern, Tennessee. All of the so mentioned cities paled in comparison to the county seat of Dyersburg – the city of 27,000 inhabitants. Dyersburg was a city that never had an accurate count of its African American citizens. The city itself had become famous for a trial of its sheriff and its judge. The scandals were so treacherous until even Dyer Countians were amazed. Dyersburg, the city that, unlike so many small southern cities, had two sides of town that traditionally housed African Americans – the Bruce Community (that had been named after Blanche Bruce, one of the first African American senators serving in U. S. Congress from the state of Mississippi from 1875 – 1881 during Reconstruction) which was located on the East side of Dyersburg and the Future City Community which was located on the West side of Dyersburg with uncertain boundaries for both. Like all other small towns within the region, Fairhaven chose Dyersburg as its model city while Dyersburg chose its neighboring cities of Jackson and Memphis as models due to the growth of these two cities.

The year was 1985.

It was Melvin's first year at Dyersburg Middle School. Melvin had graduated from Fairhaven Elementary School that served children from grades K - 7. The children had the option to attend Dyer County School System or Dyersburg City School System after seventh grade. Because Etta taught in the Dyer County School system and there were no private schools in Fairhaven for Melvin and his sisters, all of the James children were dutifully shipped to the Dyersburg City School System whereas Etta could remain partial in her judgment of educational growth of her children. As a teacher in the former system, she did not wish to become a hindrance to her children's growth and development because she was an employee, hence, the second system worked for her.

At first, Melvin was afraid to go to school in Dyersburg. He knew that transition was always hard yet it was always a necessary evil that one must face. Dyersburg Middle School was indeed much larger than Fairhaven Elementary School had been. The population of students at D.M.S. was at least three to four times larger than it had been at F.E.S. at Fairhaven, Melvin had been a star. He was not so certain about his popularity at Dyersburg Middle School.

Melvin had come to an age in his life when he realized that everything about him had begun to change. He no longer spoke in a high pitched and squeaky voice. He had begun to notice that hair had begun to sprout up in all types of places on his body... his legs, his arms, his arm pits, and even between his legs. He had also begun to realize that unlike some of his friends, he had little to no attraction to girls but had become keenly attracted to other boys. Some of his friends had gone on to become athletes and they had begun to develop muscles in all of the right places. Melvin had overheard his older sisters talking about a "gay" boy at their school. He listened intently and soon realized that, just like the gay boy in whom his sisters discussed so viciously, he had the same attraction to guys that the boy did in which they discussed.

Melvin knew that it would be hard for him to hide his sexuality at Dyersburg Middle School because he knew that there were too many fine looking boys there. He had just begun to deal with and come to grips with who he was. He had come to terms with his sexuality after passing to the sixth grade. He realized that he was naturally attracted to boys rather than girls for some strange reason that he could not really put his finger on. It was just something about the male anatomy that really turned him on. He never revealed this secret to any one, however yet he accepted the fact that he must be gay like his mother's brother, Uncle Claiborne.

Uncle Claiborne lived in Atlanta and seldom came home to Fairhaven for anything! He did not even come home for funerals. If an immediate family member died, he would come home long enough to attend the wake and leave in the wee hours of the night whereas he would miss the funeral completely yet there would always be an extremely ostentatious floral arrangement left amidst the other arrangements that always bore his insignia. At Christmas time, all of the immediate relatives received exquisitely wrapped gifts from chic shops from around the world. Grandma Bertha always received several new dresses with matching hats, furs, and elegant jewelry. Gramps Jeremiah always received two new suits with matching hats, ties, shirts, shoes, and socks. Etta always received a gift box containing the latest designer perfume while Clarence would receive a Persian sweater that he would never wear. Melvin's sisters all received new dresses from the latest designer while Melvin was always presented with a trendy new suit, new pair of Nikes, and some type of new outfit that would not become popular within that corner of Tennessee until the following year. Uncle Claiborne always sent lavish gifts but never his presence.

Time would eventually reveal its truth. Uncle Claiborne was able to make such lavish purchases each year because he was an extremely successful porn star and escort. His life afforded him a fabulous apartment in Los Angeles, a townhouse in New York City, a condo in Atlanta on the infamous Buford Highway, and a villa in Jamaica. Because of his occupation and the risk that someone from Fairhaven might confront him, he alleviated the risk by never exposing himself to the town gossip.

During locker assignment at Dyersburg Middle School, Melvin met Bradley Kelly.

Melvin had seen Bradley from afar growing up and while at church functions. Bradley was a member of Rock Spring Cumberland Presbyterian Church in America that was the family owned and built church of the Smith-Kelly Clan. Rock Spring was located in RoEllen where Bradley was from. Occasionally, Rock Spring and Mt. Carmel would fellowship in the afternoons. Both Bradley and Melvin had been choir members which only made their meeting inevitable at some point in their lives.

As destiny would have it, they were now assigned locker partners.

Soon, they discovered that they had identical schedules.

They were almost doomed to become friends or enemies.

They chose the former.

Bradley was athletic and had already begun to develop muscles. He wore a "whap" haircut. In 1983, this haircut was considered the bomb in West Tennessee. *Kid and Play* had made it famous in their movie. The haircut was simple, however. It provided the hair to be faded in the back and on the sides but the hair that remained on the top of the head was slanted to the right. Anyone who sported a "whap" would also sport, one, two, or three parts cut at varying lengths in the "whap." Bradley had a smooth, milk chocolate complexion that seemed to permeate in the sunlight. When he chose to smile, which was often, he would warm you heart instantly. Somehow, a person would always feel at ease in his presence.

At first glance, Melvin wanted him! Bradley was fine! There was indeed no doubt about that! However, after sharing a locker as well as classes with him for the entire school year, Melvin did not quite view Bradley in a romantic light any further. Instead, Bradley became the brother that Melvin never had. He was witty and he didn't mind speaking or sharing his opinion nor did he mind speaking up for himself and, occasionally, for Melvin as well. Bradley knew how to handle himself in all situations. He was a "for sure" person who definitely had his act together.

Academically, Bradley's grades matched Melvin's. Melvin was a straight "A" student and enjoyed the academic challenges that Bradley would supply his mind at times.

It was by accident that Melvin discovered Bradley's sexual preference.

The school year had soared by and had come to an end. After their fri4endship had developed and blossomed, they had become inseparable. They attended everything together. It was no surprise to see them together at church events, ball games, pep rallies, Student council meetings, school newspaper meetings, choir rehearsals, and any other activity scheduled for the middle school students. They even double dated from time to time. Melvin found this to be a little odd and silly because he knew within his own heart that he wasn't attracted to girls. He also knew that he had to "save face" in order to be accepted in the community in which he came, so he, like Bradley, would go out on dates together.

On one particular day before the end of school, the two of them overheard a group of Caucasian boys discussing pledging SPO or sigma Phi Omega Fraternity.

"Why don't we have fraternities in high school?" Melvin asked Bradley.

"We do," Bradley commented. "You haven't gotten your letter yet?

"What letter?" Melvin asked.

"A group called Omega Phi Theta sent me a letter on yesterday," Bradley said as he opened his back pack to retrieve the letter. He passed the crumpled letter to Melvin.

"I wonder why they didn't send me one?" Melvin asked a little disappointed.

"Some guy asked me about it last week. He wanted to know if I knew of any other guys who would be interested in pledging his fraternity," Bradley said quickly. "I gave them your name. You should get a letter today or tomorrow."

"Do they pledge?"

"It's a fraternity, Melvin, jeez."

"I don't know," Melvin said softly. "They might ask us to do something wrong or something."

"It's not like they are gonna ask you to suck their dick or something."

"That might be interesting," Melvin said without thinking.

"Don't I know it," Bradley said as he looked away from Melvin as if he were reminiscing of some far and distant land.

"Would you do it?" Melvin asked curiously.

"It depends on who it is," Bradley responded earnestly.

"Oh really?" Melvin commented as he attempted to lure Bradley into a long awaited question and answer. "You talk like you speak from experience or something."

"I do," Bradley commented.

"What?" Melvin was astonished.

"Huh?" Bradley said as he realized that he had revealed his secret. "Well, what's wrong?"

"I'm just shocked," Melvin confessed.

"Shocked about what?" Bradley asked.

"That you've done it," Melvin commented earnestly. "I've always wanted to try it but I don't really know nobody in Fairhaven."

Bradley inhaled and released a long yet slow gush of air. He forgot that he often aimlessly drifted into a world of his own. Whenever he did this, the world became oblivious to him. Now, he had revealed a secret about himself. He did not mind Melvin knowing but he was not always comfortable around Melvin. Melvin could sometimes have such a serene and peaceful aura about himself until Bradley felt that it was either angelic or judgmental. Now, Bradley was looking at his best friend and openly declaring that he wanted or have had sex with another boy. This was becoming more sordid than Bradley ever anticipated. Here it was that Melvin lived a life whereas he managed to have everything. It was not so with Bradley. He had to scuffle in order to help keep food on the table at times. He knew that his mother was an alcoholic. His father had been gone since he was six or seven. He could not quite remember. Through it all, though, he had managed to keep his head held high. He soon found himself blessed to have become a friend of Melvin's although Melvin could sometimes get on another level than where he was at.

Bradley looked into Melvin's eyes.

Melvin actually lost the serenity about his aura and began to look rather pitiful in Bradley's opinion.

"So, are you saying that you are gay or what?" Bradley questioned.

"I guess I am," Melvin confessed in a manner that seemed to be a relief. His eyes rolled into the back of his head as a smile began to develop across his face. "Are you?"

"If that's what you wanna call it," Bradley chuckled. "I call it having fun."

"Well, I've never been with anybody but I'm a little curious" Melvin admitted.

"Well, you'd better not go public with this new found revelation and try to find somebody or you'll be ruined in high school," Bradley advised.

"Well," Melvin wondered aloud. "Who have you been with then since you are such an expert?"

Melvin had suddenly become fascinated with this aspect of his friend Bradley's life. This new revelation made him admire and idolize Bradley all the more. Over the period of a year's time, Bradley had become the brother that Melvin had always wanted but never had. They had become inseparable but Melvin was almost insulted that Bradley had not revealed this insatiable secret about himself. Now, it seemed as if they had embarked upon a new beginning all together which only made their friendship solidify in a totally new aspect.

"If you tell this, I won't ever speak to you again," Bradley said plainly as he looked squarely into Melvin's eyes to search for truth and understanding. "Plus, I'll kick your ass from here to China!"

"Have I ever told any of our secrets?" Melvin questioned as he thought about all of the things they had secretly conspired to do together if it was nothing more than stealing an archenemy's books and hiding them the day before a major assignment was due.

"Did you ever know the Curbies from Fairhaven?" Bradley asked.

"I don't know them very well," Melvin admitted as his heart began to pound. Joshua Curbie and Jeremy Curbie were two brothers who occasionally attended Mt. Carmel in Fairhaven. Josh was tall, slender, and had a swimmer's build. Jeremy was tall, stocky and had a football players build. Both were known in Fairhaven for their athletic abilities. Both of them were honey yellow in complexion and both sported Jherri curls. Josh, by 1986, had enjoyed a very successful athletic career at Dyer County High School and had landed a football scholarship at Georgia Tech University in Atlanta, Georgia. Jeremy, a much better athlete than Josh, was enjoying a wonderful senior year at Dyer County High School in Newbern, Tennessee whereas scouts from the NFL, NBA, and various colleges and universities courted his decision to play for their teams. Because Melvin had not really been athletically inclined, he never really hung out with either of them partially because both were jocks and because he was younger, they never shared much of the same interests.

"Well," Bradley began as he recounted the night in question. "Last December, Momma dropped me off at the Curbies house while she and Trish Ann decided to go out."

This was no surprise to anyone who knew Bradley's family. His mother, Delores Kelly, was indeed a worldly woman in every sense of the word. It was no secret that she would leave Bradley at a relative or neighbor's house for weeks at a time while she went on a party venge or "midnight rendezvous." No one really knew where she went but many people had their own suspicions. A person does not leave home broke and return several days later with an uncertain amount of money. Delores did. Delores also dared anyone to "get into her business" for fear that she would stab the perpetrator. Delores was not an ugly woman but she was not pretty either. She would be considered common or plain in her looks. She seldom wore clothing that made her appear to look feminine yet when she did wear them; she looked totally different and actually looked better than what she portrayed to the world on a daily basis. These ere the times that people did not know who she was. She loved Bradley but she only knew how to do nothing more than provide him with the mere basics... food, shelter, and always nice clothing. She actually treated Bradley more like a brother than her actual child. When people saw them together, the mother-son relationship that they had established would definitely melt the heart of anyone who saw them together. Bradley never questioned what Delores did when she left for days at a time. He made up in his mind years ago not to even care. He figured that his mother had to do what she had to do in order to provide for him unlike his father.

Trish Ann Curbie was altogether a different story. Trish Ann's house was in constant chaos. She was a tiny woman in stature who had a face that seemed as if it had been sculpted by the gods themselves. Many people had often questioned why she never chose modeling as an occupation. Unfortunately, Trish Ann, in all of her beauty, sometimes seemed like the village idiot in her logical approach to life, especially when choosing men. She had five children in which she raised alone. When the opportunity presented itself, she attended Mt. Carmel and was one of the best singers that the choir had but she could not remain committed for long periods of time to the choir. By the age of fifteen, she had been impregnated with her first child by her high school sweet heart, Joshua Thomas Fields or J.T. as he was nicknamed. Trish Ann therefore named her first born after his father and the world was introduced to Joshua Allen Fields. J.T. had promised to marry Trish Ann after they graduated high school and she fell for the reasoning that he gave her. At the time, the United States was engage in the Vietnam War and J.T. had been drafted to serve his country. As time would have it, Trish Ann became pregnant with her second child soon before her eighteenth birthday and the world was introduced to Jeremy Alex Fields. J.T. was killed in action shortly after the birth of Jeremy. Grievously, Trish Ann then began dating James Beauregard "J.B." Washington who provided her with yet another child in which they named James Beauregard Washington, Junior. After J.B. Junior was born, J.B., Senior decided that it was time for him to return home to his wife who lived in Lauderdale County. Heartbroken and distraught, Trish Ann then met King Davis Curbie. Mister "Kang" owned a store in Trenton,

Tennessee and one in Fairhaven. Trish Ann was in heaven. She had finally met a man who loved her for beyond her physical beauty and actually was interested in her thoughts as well. King moved his new family to Trenton, adopted all of the children, and then married Trish Ann. King's mother hated Trish Ann yet after the birth of Erica and Jessica, her first twins, the mother-in-law changed her tune somewhat. King gave Trish Ann every desire of her heart. Just when she felt that life was going great for herself, king was killed in a car accident coming home from the store one night. Heartbroken and distraught again, Trish Ann moved back to Dyer County; bought a double wide trailer in Fairhaven; and moved her family back there. Trish Ann abandoned the store that was located in Trenton and gave it to her mother-in-law while she half heartedly operated the store that King owned in Fairhaven.

Delores Kelly and Trish Ann Curbie had been best friends since grammar school and as adulthood settled they managed to maintain a friendship. On this particular autumn night, they had decided that they needed a break from being parents. They needed a "girl's night out" in order to get away from the harsh realities of life. Because Josh was the eldest child, he was placed in charge of the care of all of the children. Since Bradley could take care of himself, he was ushered to Trish Ann's house for safe keeping until Delores returned. Josh always resented being placed in charge of the pack but he would always comply quickly or get a prompt and thorough beating from Trish Ann who, although short and petite, could inflict the worse type of pain and punishment on any of her children at any time it was deemed necessary.

By the time Delores had pulled into Trish Ann's driveway of her trailer, all of the children were asleep except for Josh who had been enlisted as the "baby-sitter." Bradley begrudgingly walked up the steps as Trish Ann walked out. Delores had turned the music inside of the car up and the sweet chords of "Misty Blue" rang out into the night and could be heard through ought the trailer. Fortunately, none of the sleeping children woke up.

"Well, what da ya wanna do?" Josh asked as the car sped off into the night with the two women cackling like schoolgirls.

"I don't know," Bradley said as he walked into the house and sat down on the sofa and began to stare aimlessly at the television.

"You wanna drank of beer?" Josh asked as he went to the refrigerator door, opened it up, and rambled around inside of it until he found a bottle of Schlitz Malt Liquor beer.

"Naw, I'm all right," Bradley said as he continued to stare aimlessly at the television.

"Hey, you wanna watch a tape?" Josh asked as he grabbed the remote to the television and VCR and then plopped down in a seat beside Bradley on the sofa.

"Sure," Bradley said with such lack of enthusiasm that he could not wake a comatose person. Bradley had become bored with the entire interlude and was actually preparing his mind to go to sleep. He could, however, sense that something great was about to happen to him yet he could not put his finger on it. Secretly, he had a crush on Josh but Josh always seemed too preoccupied with girls and football. Over the years, he had made Josh his idol and secretly enjoyed the few moments that he could spend with him on nights like this. Although Bradley was a few years younger than Josh, Josh had always made time for him as well as all of the other younger boys within the community. Now, however, Bradley had begun to feel weird in Josh's presence. It was as if josh had begun to permeate a side of his soul that had been untapped.

Josh ran into his bedroom and retrieved a tattered video tape. He closed the bedroom door where a snoring Jeremy laid and a sleeping JB was opposite him in a second bed. In another bedroom, Josh peeped in to see the twins were also fast asleep. They were and he closed their bedroom door as well.

The video tape did not have a name on it. It looked ragged and well worn with time.

"You sure you can handle dis?" Josh asked as he placed the worn videotape into the VCR and then sat down immediately beside Bradley.

"Yeah," Bradley lied.

Josh adjusted the television set's volume whereas the two of them could vaguely hear the music and words that came from the video yet it would not disturb the sleeping children in the other rooms. Suddenly, a man appeared on the television screen. The man was screwing the woman with such vigor until Bradley's eyes almost popped out of their sockets in mere shock at what he was now viewing with his idol. He had heard about this type of video but had never seen one before.

Josh noticed that Bradley had become uncomfortable and suddenly a wicked smile appeared on his face.

"You sure you don't want no beer?" Josh asked.

"Yeah," Bradley replied as he continued to watch the video. His nerves had become unsettled and a bulge had begun to rise between his legs. The woman was moaning as the man had begun to pound her. This had really begun to unsettle Bradley. "I think I'll have some."

Josh stood up, went to the refrigerator, and grabbed the beer from within. He poured Bradley a glass and then refilled his own. He decided to bring the quart of beer to the sofa and sit it down on the coffee table nearby whereas they could drink as much as they liked at liberty.

He placed a glass of beer into Bradley's hand. Bradley immediately gulped down several swallows before Josh could return to his seat next to him.

"Nervous?" Josh asked as he sat down much closer beside Bradley than he had previously been.

"Not really," Bradley lied as he gulped down another sip of beer. A new scene appeared on the television screen. A woman had begun to suck the sex organ of the man who was obviously the star of the movie. Bradley kept his eyes glued to the television set although his skin had begun to feel tingly.

"Damn," Josh commented as he watched the television screen and then the reactions of Bradley. "Dat looks good,"

"Umm hmm," Bradley commented as he took another large gulp of beer which, consequently, was his last.

"Slow down, man," Josh growled. "Damn!"

"Sorry," Bradley said nervously. "I just never saw a tape like this before."

"Ah, it ain't nothin'," josh said as he poured more beer into Bradley's glass. Bradley began to watch the movie now with greater interest. The star of the movie had one of the biggest organs he had ever seen in his life. It had begun to fascinate him. Once again, the star had begun to slide his organ down the throat of yet another female.

"I be t dat feels real good," Josh whispered as he slowly sipped his beer.

"Looks like it would hurt to me," Bradley responded absently.

"How would you know?" Josh asked slyly. "Have you ever tried it?"

"No," Bradley answered honestly.

"I bet you could suck a mean dick," Josh said matter-of-factly.

A sweat broke out on Bradley's forehead. He didn't know what to do or what to say. He liked Josh and always had. Secretly, he had fantasized about what an experience would be like with Josh but never had he ever dreamed they would come into fruition. Now, josh was saying all of these things.

"Why, why, why would you say that?" Bradley stuttered as he nervously asked the question. For the first time during the entire conversation, Bradley noticed that Josh had a lump that was seemingly getting bigger between his legs.

"You got pretty lips," Josh replied in a soft yet sexy whisper that really began to unnerve Bradley at this point.

"I,I,I, don't know about all that," Bradley said a bit nervous but attempting to make the conversation more interesting. "I'm sure you've seen prettier in you day, Mr. Athlete. Plus, I ain't never done nothing like this before anyway."

"Have you ever wanted to?" Josh asked.

This floored Bradley.

Hell yes he had wanted to. Many, many, many times before he had fantasized about Josh whenever he came over to Trish Ann's house. Josh and Jeremy would be wrestling without shirts on. Both were terribly fine but Josh had always appealed to Bradley while Jeremy never quite did it for him. Josh was muscular but had a tight swimmer's build. Jeremy, although slender as well, was also muscular but had more of a wrestler's build somewhat like Muhammad Ali but just taller.

He actually wanted to do this very thing that he saw on the video to Josh!

"I never thought about it," Bradley lied. In truth, however, he had prayed for this moment for years and was taken back slightly because it was actually occurring. Now that the moment had finally come, Bradley had actually become afraid.

"Do you like me, Brad?" Josh asked as he moved closer to Bradley.

"Yeah, you know I do, Josh," Bradley confessed. "You used to be all of our hero when we were growing up but when you got to high school you changed and didn't have time for us anymore."

"It's not that I didn't have time for you," Josh said as his hand began to move up Bradley's leg and gently caress it. "I just been tryin' hard to get me a scholarship to play ball somewhere and I gotta practice, dat's all. You know I'll always have time for y'all... especially you!"

"Oh," Bradley said as he sipped his beer.

"Yeah," Josh said as he began to move his hand upward toward Bradley's sex organ. He gently caressed it which made it fully erect. Bradley wanted some type of relief because his sex was so hard until it was beginning to hurt him. Josh was beginning to say and do all of these things and the people on the video were really going at it now.

"Brad, would you do me a favor?" Josh asked.

"Sure, what?"

"Let me see your thang."

Bradley almost lost his breath in shock and disbelief. Was hearing this right? Josh wanted to see his aching *thang*?

"Why?" Bradley managed to whisper.

"Just let me see it," Josh demanded.

"O.K." Bradley whispered as he slipped his pants and underwear down around his waist fully exposing his massive yet fully erect sex organ. Before he could say anything, Josh had completely engulfed Bradley's sex organ within his warm and moist lips. The impact of Josh's lips around his sex sent Bradley into a state of shock and ecstasy at the same time. He had never before experienced this type of pleasure and it was good, good, good!

"You like dat?" Josh asked as he came up for air momentarily.

"Yea, yeah, yes," Bradley moaned as he could barely whisper the words from his mouth.

"Pull your pants off and lie on your back completely then," josh said as he began to try to pull Bradley's pants off. Bradley resisted, however. Suddenly, fear struck him

"What if somebody comes in here?" Bradley asked as his eyes began to slightly widen as the reality of his verbal thought came into perspective. He wondered just what would be said and possibly done if he and josh were caught in this act that the preacher so vehemently preached about on a regular basis.

"O.K." Josh said. "Then let's go to my room. I got a lock on my door."

Bradley quickly pulled his underwear and pants up. Josh stood up, removed the video from the VCR and placed it in the back of his pants; grabbed the empty glasses and the slightly empty beer bottle; and proceeded into this bedroom. Bradley followed him.

When inside of the bedroom, Josh told Bradley to pull off all of his clothes and lie down on the bed. Bradley followed his instructions. Josh locked the bedroom door and moved closer to the bed beside Bradley who had become an extremely nervous wreck in bewilderment as to what was going to transpire.

"You want me to sex you up, baby?" Josh whispered.

"Yeah," Bradley whimpered as he lay back on the fluffy pillow that was at the head of Josh's bed. Josh removed his clothes and revealed a perfectly chiseled body to Bradley. He then crawled into bed and nestled atop of Bradley. Josh began to lick Bradley's neck, his chest, his stomach, his belly button, and then he began to tease him. Josh would lick toward the top of Bradley's sex organ; nibble quickly; and then move quickly to the side of Bradley's leg, his balls, or anywhere except his sex organ. This began to drive Bradley mad with ecstasy. He had never experienced such an emotion as he had begun to experience now with Josh. He never wanted this to end yet at the same time he wanted Josh to go ahead and suck his sex organ.

"Tell me what you want me to do, baby?" josh teased.

"Suck my ding-a-ling," Bradley said in the sexiest voice that he could muster all the while trying to sound grown up. To his complete and utter amazement, josh sat straight up and began to laugh so hard until Bradley began to stare at him in bewilderment. Bradley could not understand what had happened. Was all of this some type of twisted joke to see how far he would go?

"What I say?" Bradley questioned earnestly. He wanted to do the right thing yet it had become a complete joke to Josh and this began to make him angry and he was not above fighting if he had to.

"Suck your ding-a-ling," Josh laughed. "I haven't heard that in years."

"Then what am I supposed to call it?" Bradley asked.

"Suck my dick," Josh said matter-of-factly. "Is that what ya want?"

"Yeah."

"Then say it!" Josh growled.

"Suck my dick, nigga," Bradley spat out.

Before Bradley could move, Josh was all over it which caused Bradley to arch his back and fall backwards onto the bed moaning, groaning, and grinding his hips in the rhythm of Josh's expert lips and the motion of his head. Words could not express the feelings that soared and raged throughout Bradley's body as Josh did this wonderful and exciting thing to him. Before he realized it, Bradley had a firm grip on Josh's head. He began to shake and shiver as he held Josh's head tighter and closer to him. Soon, he could not help himself. He began to cum inside of Josh's mouth while he continued to hold a strong yet firm grip on Josh's head which forced Josh closer to him.

Josh squirmed and managed to break free of the hold that Bradley had on him.

"Got damn it, nigga," Josh growled and began to spit. "Ya tryin' to kill me?"

Bradley could not answer Josh nor could he move as his body continued to shake and shiver.

Josh jumped up and ran to his closet, retrieved a towel, and came back to the bed where Bradley lay trembling. Bradley could hear Josh in a litany of spitting into a nearby waste basket.

Bradley looked at Josh in bewilderment as Josh wiped the remaining cum from Bradley's leg. He also noticed that Josh's monstrous looking "dick" was fully erect and definitely standing at attention.

Josh noticed how Bradley was in awe of his sex organ.

A wicked smile appeared on Josh's face as he continued to stare at Bradley.

"Ya wanna help me out now?" Josh asked.

"I guess so," Bradley replied nervously. He had never really done anything like this before yet here he was lying naked as a jay bird in the bed with his childhood hero about to suck the first dick he had ever encountered in his life. Before Bradley could say another word, Josh grabbed his head and began to pump his organ into his mouth. Being a quick study of the video and Josh's previous performance, Bradley attempted to do things to Josh that Josh had done to him plus add a few things that he had seen on the video. He apparently did a good job because Josh began to moan, groan, and even yell as Bradley began to suck harder and faster.

"Hell, yeah, do dat," Josh groaned. "Yeah, dats right, suck dat motha fuckin dick!"

Pleased by his performance, Bradley began to attempt to swallow the entire shaft but before he knew exactly what was going on, he felt Josh's organ become slightly larger and then an explosion of white gook began inside of his mouth whereas he released the shaft and even more of it squirted out onto his face.

"Got damn, nigga," Josh roared. "Oh this shit is so fuckin good!"

"Yes!" Bradley smirked triumphantly to himself. *"I made him cum! I must have done something right!"*

Bradley spit the contents of what was inside of his mouth into the waste basket next to the bed that Josh had spit into previously.

"How was it?" Bradley asked.

"Real good," Josh panted. "It was so good in fact looka here."

Bradley looked between Josh's legs only to discover that Josh still had a hard on. At this point, he didn't' know what to expect.

"Ya still got me going, baby," Josh said. "Come over here and let's do the nasty."

Bradley complied and lie beside Josh on the bed. Bradley really didn't know what the "nasty" was but he had a good idea. Soon, Josh began to message his buttocks.

"Turn over on your stomach," josh instructed.

Bradley obediently turned onto his stomach.

Bradley heard the lid of a jar that sat on a nightstand beside the bed being opened.

Josh began to rub some type of grease onto the whole of his butt. He tried to relax as Josh's finger began to invade his private part but he could not. He began to squirm and twist.

"Be still," Josh growled.

Bradley remained as still as he possibly could get.

Soon, Bradley could feel the head of Josh's organ push down into him. *"So this is the nasty?"* Bradley thought as pain began to permeate his body such that tears began to stream down his face. He wanted to please Josh but he was not so certain if he wanted to please

Josh *this* much. Yet, there was nowhere to run in order to get away from the pain. He was trapped underneath this guy who was beginning to invade his insides.

Bradley's heart began to race as Josh began to slowly pull out of him and then thrust back into him.

"God, if the pain will just stop," Bradley thought to himself as he attempted to remain as still as possible as Josh continued this invasion of his virgin body.

"Just relax," Josh whispered in his ear and began to kiss his neck and the side of his face that was soaked in tears at this point. "I promise you the pain will go away in just a minute."

Surely enough, as Josh began a slow rhythm, the pain began to subside and Bradley began to experience yet another new sensation and pleasure that he had never experienced before. The feeling began to become pleasurable and Bradley found himself moving to the slow rhythm that Josh had begun. Josh flipped him over from on his stomach and onto his back. Bradley began to moan, groan, grunt, and growl as josh continued the litany. Bradley began to like it so much until he grabbed Josh's waist and began to pull Josh's body forward into him. Josh had not expected this to go so well. Soon, Bradley yelled out Josh's name as he began to rock back and forth to every thrust that Josh gave him.

The excitement of it all was all too much for Josh.

"I'm cummin," Josh screamed.

"Oh yes, give it to me, baby," Bradley yelled as he held onto Josh with a grip that was so tight until it took the wind out of Josh.

After this, they both fell quickly asleep.

The next day, Delores and Trish Ann arrived home from a long night out. Bradley went home with his mother satisfied. The encounters and adventures that he had with Josh became legendary events in both of their lives. Their association and liaison lasted long after Josh had graduated high school.

"How in the hell did you manage to do all of that?" Melvin asked in sheer awe of Bradley.

"Josh said that I was just a natural talent," Bradley giggled.

"I bet he did," Melvin smirked. "When did all of this occur and how long has it been going on?"

"We started about two years ago before Josh went off to college," Bradley bragged. "We still get together occasionally whenever he comes home."

"You poor thing," Melvin teased. "Now you don't have a boyfriend."

"Boyfriend my ass," Bradley laughed. "Hell, I'm glad he's gone!"

"Why?"

"Because I'm dating somebody from Milan and somebody else from Humboldt and I really did get tired of Josh."

"When did you have time to do all of this, hussy?"

"Well," Bradley giggled. "I met one guy at the General Assembly last year and I met the other one at the Sunday School Convention this past summer."

For the first time ever, Bradley was able to share a portion of his secret life with somebody else. He had never been able to do this prior to this moment. It was amazing to him that finally he was actually telling somebody besides God about his triumphs and his joys; his loves and his heartbreaks; and of course, his many conquests. This made him feel proud to be Melvin's friend and prayed the feelings were mutual.

"Isn't General Assembly like our Congress?" Melvin asked as he attempted to understand the separate rules of the Cumberland Presbyterian Church in America versus the Christian Methodist Episcopal Church versus the African Methodist Episcopal Church versus the Church of God in Christ versus the National Baptist Convention in which he was affiliated. To Melvin, the rules and regulations of the National Baptist Convention, U.S.A., Incorporated were far easier to understand than with the other denominations. Melvin could not even imagine sitting under the jurisdiction of a

Bishop and so on and so forth. Bradley was born into a family who had founded one of the Cumberland Presbyterian Churches within the Hew Hopewell Presbytery, hence, it was all that he had ever been exposed to religiously except for the fellowship with the various other churches and denominations. His mother, Delores, had been raised Christian Methodist Episcopal but upon marrying into the Smith-Kelly Clan, had joined her husband's religion until their divorce.

"You all's Congress is more like our Sunday School Convention," Bradley explained. "General Assembly is more like you all's Association."

"O.K." Melvin responded, still a bit confused but wanting to change the subject. "So, what is this fraternity stuff all about anyway?"

"You'll get a letter this week."

"How do you know?"

"Consideration is based on your grades and your social standing," Bradley explained. "Believe me, we have both."

"What will they do if they find out about us?" Melvin asked as his eyes began to bulge with fear of becoming discovered.

"Hell," Bradley chuckled. "Just don't fuck none of them and you'll be all right."

"What if one of them tries to fuck me?" Melvin asked.

"It will be an experience of a lifetime," Bradley chuckled. "Believe that!"

Melvin did receive an invitation to pledge The Omega Phi Theta Fraternity just as Bradley had predicted. His letter awaited his arrival home on that afternoon.

The Zeta Phi Chapter of The Omega Phi Theta Fraternity was indeed no joke in 1986. It was a fraternity of high school young men. They were African American and proud to be such. The organization had managed to become a charted organization within the State of

Tennessee in 1984 and lived a chivalrous code of ethics which boasted their motto of brotherhood, unity, and loyalty until death. Omega Phi Theta or OPT was formed in 1980 by twelve African American high school students in protest of the Sigma Phi Omega Fraternity. Sigma Phi Omega was an all Caucasian high school fraternity located in Dyersburg and Ripley, Tennessee just as Alpha Delta Kappa was an all Caucasian sorority located in the respective cities. In 1979, the Dyersburg Alumnae Chapter of the Delta Sigma Theta Sorority had commissioned a junior sorority named Delta Tau Nu Sorority for its high school African American females. In 1980, an African American young man approached Sigma Phi Omega or SPO Fraternity and asked if he could pledge and why was it that there were no African Americans in SPO? The response to his question was simple: "It is an unofficial rule of SPO that we do not pledge blacks!" This infuriated the young man. He, along with twelve other young men consulted a member of Omega Psi Phi Fraternity on how to organize and form a fraternity. Because of legalities, Omega Psi Phi could not sponsor a junior fraternity, however, the "Que" served as an advisor of the twelve in the founding of The Omega Phi Theta Fraternity. The Delta Tau Nu Sorority surnamed the Deltines teamed up with the new fraternity to form the Zeta Phi Chapter and in 1980 The Zeta Phi Chapter of the Omega Phi Theta Fraternity and the Zeta Phi Chapter of the Delta Tau Nu Sorority were formed in Dyersburg, Tennessee. The Dyersburg Alumnae Chapter of The Delta Sigma Theta Sorority, Inc. served as sponsors and advisors for The Zeta Phi Chapter of The Delta Tau Nu Sorority while The Zeta Phi Chapter of The Omega Phi Theta Fraternity had a member of the Omega Psi Phi Fraternity and a local postman as their advisors.

The two organizations became a beacon of youth activity within the African American communities of Dyer County, Tennessee. Hence, the previous trend of the only fraternity or sorority within Dyer County offered to the youth was that of Sigma Phi Omega Fraternity or the Alpha Delta Kappa Sorority came to an end at the turn of 1980. Many African American high school youth went to great lengths to become members of these two organizations.

By 1985, however, dissention arose in Omega Phi Theta due partially to an enormous growth spurt which only caused a thirst for power. This thirst caused the fraternity to split. The effects of the split caused the founding of a separate fraternity, The Kappa League. Because many of the members of the Delta Tau Nu Sorority dated members of the newly formed Kappa League, the sorority pulled out of the Zeta Phi Chapter.

OPT and the Kappa League became the major topic of all teenage discussion during the summer of 1985. The Kappa League hit the city of Dyersburg by storm in their red and white. O.P.T., with its six members, sat by and said nor did anything yet they merely watched this new organization as well as the activities of SPO. Eventually, the newness of the Kappa League wore off and OPT hit the entire area like a hurricane.

After the split of 1985, Omega Phi Theta was left only with six members but by the beginning of autumn, the fraternity boasted of seven chapters that spread across the West Tennessee area. The very first Banquet for Parents occurred in September followed by the first Halloween Carnival in October followed by the first Miss Omega Phi Theta Beauty Pageant in November followed by the New Year's Eve Ball in December. Both the Kappa League and the Deltines were left in awe of the diligence and determination of the six members who had remained in Omega Phi Theta.

Both Melvin and Bradley were presented with an ultimatum upon consideration of pledging OPT. Because the Kappa League had fought OPT both tooth and nails for membership, OPT had adopted a new slogan: "Quality not Quantity in OPT!" all new candidates for member of OPT went through an extensive interview process before even being considered for the role as pledges on line. Loyalty was a key quality that the "old guard" looked for in its new members. On the line of 1986 in Dyer County, only family members of the six "old guard" were allowed to pledge. If they were not kin to the members of the "old guard" they were permitted to pledge only if they were members of Dyer County African American Elite families. Anyone else was excluded. The "Old Guard" refused to endure another split within the history of the fraternity and time ensured that a split never occurred again.

When Melvin and Bradley discovered that the "Old Guard" had denied several applications, they began to have second thoughts about pledging. Nevertheless, Melvin found himself at the Bruce Community Center on one sunny April afternoon sitting in the conference room in front of a long desk with six African American young men sizing him up. Those six men asked a series of long and tedious questions only to ensure that Melvin was indeed "O.P.T. material."

"What is your grade point average?" a tall yet slender guy nicknamed *The Rev* asked. He seemed to have some type of vendetta against anything that moved. He was an attractive guy with a very prominent facial structure. His lips were full, his cheekbones were high yet dimpled, and his eyebrows were thick yet straight across his forehead. He fashionably wore a shoulder length Jherri curl that surprisingly never dripped onto his clothes. His clothes were a neat arrangement of the latest business attire.

"3.865," Melvin replied and chose the floor to look at rather than panel who were interviewing him.

"The question was addressed to you, Mr. James," The Rev began. "We would appreciate it if you would address this panel and not the floor from this point on."

"*This is obviously the bitch of the group,*" Melvin thought yet replied. "Yes, sir."

"How would you explain a belief in brotherhood, unity, and loyalty?" a stocky brother nicknamed Grimlock questioned. Grimlock was also a very handsome man. He had a smooth yet dark complexion, piercing eyes, and a very contagious smile that revealed a set of white teeth that had definitely seen great dental care. Although formal, he was not quite as stuffy as The Rev was. His disposition was rather jovial in comparison which tended to make one feel comfortable and at ease within his presence.

"Brotherhood," Melvin said as he began to choose his words both wisely and carefully as he looked at the six men on the panel. "is what I see before me right now. I see six young black men who will be there for each other no matter what. I see six young black men who, against the odds, forged a major fraternity network across the great state of Tennessee. I also see six young black men who will go to great lengths to make certain that there are no weak links trying to invade what is so precious to them."

"Well put," a squinty-eyed brother nicknamed Light Bulb grinned. Light bulb had a perpetual grin that made you think of the Cheshire cat. Like the others, Light Bulb was quite debonair which made him attractively handsome. His style was very polished yet it differed greatly from The Rev's style of fashion. His features reminded a person of an Indian prince or a warrior from Persia. He was, Melvin learned, the President of the organization. With The Rev in the room, however, Melvin wondered how Light Bulb held this position. He was sure that he would discover it as time progressed along. Melvin did notice, however, that Light Bulb would give The Rev a certain glance when he desired The Rev to shut up and The Rev would comply immediately and without a word of complaint. Melvin wondered what type of hold Light bulb had on The Rev. "Now would you explain unity and loyalty to us, you have covered brotherhood pretty good in my opinion."

The members of the panel nodded in agreement to Light bulb's words.

"Again," Melvin began his litany of praise of the "Old Guard" as instructed and advised by Bradley. "When I look at how unified you gentlemen are, I am at a loss of words..." Bradley had insisted that all he had to do was constantly flatter them and they would suck the flattery up as if they were sopping molasses from a biscuit.

"For goodness sakes, skip the bullshit and tell us what you really think or what your definition of unity and loyalty is, man!" grumbled a very impatient brother nicknamed Petey. Just when Melvin thought that he had already met *"The Evil One"* when he had met The Rev, Petey woke up from what seemed to be either a long daze or a long sleep with his eyes open. Petey was a short, bald, slightly dumpy, dark skinned guy who definitely had an attitude problem. Sometimes his arrogant aura would visibly cause a slight friction between the members of the panel. "We know who we are and we know what you want! Now what the hell do *you* think, man?"

"I think that you are an asshole and you really don't want to know what the hell I think," Melvin thought to himself but decided not to

falter from his relentless pursuit of flatter in order to gain the acceptance and approval of these men who obviously had their acts together. "Again, unity is when brothers can come together and nothing can separate them."

"O.K., then what is your definition of loyalty?" a familiar looking guy nicknamed Skull asked. Melvin recognized Skull because skull was a very popular and recognized football hero within both Dyer County and Shelby County, Tennessee. Like the others, Skull was also a very attractive young man who had a freshly cut haircut, a butterball head, thin yet surprisingly pink lips, and muscles everywhere. He indeed looked like a football player.

"When you will die for something," Melvin answered earnestly.

"Will you die for this fraternity?" a tall, dark, and slender brother nicknamed The Shaw asked and burst into extreme laughter. His laughter had such a shrill pitch to it until it became contagious amongst the panel. All of the brothers laughed yet Melvin sat and stared blankly at them all. *"These are truly idiots indeed,"* he thought.

"If it is required," he replied.

Immediately the laughter ceased.

"May I have a motion to end this interview," Light Bulb asked hurriedly.

"So moved," Petey responded.

For the first time during the interview, Melvin noticed The Rev as he quickly scribbled something on a note pad that was almost completely full of scribbling. Melvin then realized that the entire interview had been recorded by The Rev.

"Second the motion," Grimlock chimed in.

"Mr. James, we thank you for your time and great effort in contributing to this interview. This concludes this portion of the interview process. Within the next couple of days you should receive a statement in the mail concerning your application status…" The Rev monotonously yet formally stated before being interrupted by Light Bulb.

"One last question, Mr. James," Light Bulb interrupted The Rev which caused The Rev's left eyebrow to arch up and his head to slightly turn in Light Bulb's direction who sat to his immediate left. It almost seemed as if The Rev was about to curse Light Bulb out yet he remained silent as his lips pursed. "We note that you are not from Dyersburg. If you were given a post out in Fairhaven do you feel that you are qualified to fill any position given you?"

"If you note in my application, Mr. President," Melvin smirked. "You will see that I have successfully presided over several organizations prior to applying for this one..."

"Thank you, Mr. James, that will be all," The Rev interrupted Melvin before any further comment could be made by him or the panel. Melvin could almost feel the tension within the room as Skull and Petey led him to the door and escorted him out of the room.

"I guess that put smoke in your pipe," Melvin thought wickedly to himself. *"I wouldn't give a crap if those idiots never called me to pledge OPT even though I hear that it is the frat to be in when I get to high school next year."*

As soon as Melvin arrived home he immediately telephoned Bradley. The interview with O.P.T. had unsettled him slightly; hence, he needed some type of reassurance from his best friend that he had said the *right* things during the interview. Those guys did not look pleased at all with his last comments yet he had said them. They also looked like they did not play in anyone's mess. It almost seemed funny that this fraternity was supposed to be the best fraternity of the two African American fraternities within the Dyer County area. Melvin already knew that to pledge SPO was not even an option or consideration. AS night settled, Melvin began to desire to become a member of O.P.T. although he also realized that the fraternity structure was more Dyersburg oriented. He began to wonder why these people would want pledges from Fairhaven, RoEllen or Newbern.

"Hello," Bradley answered the telephone on the second ring as normal.

"What did you think about the interview?" Melvin questioned.

"Oh, I don't know," Bradley said. "It seems as if they only want Dyersburg people in that particular frat to me. Even though I'm kin to one of the members, I don't think I'll be picked."

"If you're kin to one of those guys, you'll get in," Melvin said tartly as he thought about how dry and stuffy they all appeared during the interview session.

"I don't know about that," Bradley insisted. "I think they are planning something major for this area. Did you notice how many people were there from RoEllen, Newbern, and Fairhaven?"

"I really didn't pay it any attention," Melvin admitted.

"Either they are interviewing more than one day or something is up," Bradley contended.

"We'll see," Melvin commented. "We'll see!"

Three days later both Melvin and Bradley received letters of acceptance for pledging and were given directions to report to the Bruce Community Center in Dyersburg, Tennessee on April 30th for further instructions.

"Did you get your letter?" Bradley yelled into the telephone as Melvin picked up on the first ring.

"In my hand," Melvin giggled. "Well, we made the interview stage and now here comes the pledging part."

"Just remember, Melvin," Bradley advised. "It's all just a mind game."

"How do you know?"

"I got it from a secret source," Bradley commented.

"Who?" Melvin questioned.

"Don't you worry about it," Bradley said coyly. "You just remember it's all a big mind game."

"You haven't had one of the members have you?" Melvin questioned suspiciously.

"And if I have?"

"Well no wonder you got picked!"

"How dare you," Bradley raged. "Why would I have to sleep with someone in order to pledge a fucking *high school* fraternity? I know I gets mine and all but you just remember, Melvin James, I do have a relative in the damned fraternity. I may not be wealthy and all of that shit but The Smith-Kelly Clan reaches far and wide and we takes care of one another."

Melvin realized that he had offended his friend yet it was truly unintentional. He did not like that. He realized that Bradley did everything within his power to fit into the social circles that Melvin was basically born into. Bradley's mother always attempted to undermine any efforts that he made in becoming successful. It was Melvin who had basically taken Bradley under his wing and made sure that he would fit into Dyer County's Elite Black Society.

"Look, Brad," Melvin said softly as Bradley continued to rage. "I wasn't implying that you had to sleep with anyone in order to get into the fraternity. I'm still unsettled with why is it that all of us from the country are being asked to pledge this city fraternity. Not all of us who were there for the interview even attend Dyersburg high School, you know?"

"Well," Bradley said shortly. "Something must be up."

"I'm sure that it is."

"I wouldn't worry about it either way."

"O.K." Melvin said. "I won't."

On May 1, 1986, Melvin James and Bradley Kelly arrived on Vernon Street in Dyersburg, Tennessee at The Bruce Community Recreation Center as instructed by the letter. When they arrived, they were shocked to see the turnout of people who had actually made line. There were forty people to be exact!

"From this point on, you are no longer considered anything or will be referred to as anything except a Mutt! I, and any other *member* of Omega Phi Theta is to be referred to as Big Brother until June first! I am Big Brother Skull to you and it's going to be a pleasure kicking you off line and never seeing your miserable faces again!" Big Brother Skull growled as he looked into the eyes of each and every pledge. "If anybody wants to walk, get to steppin' right now."

Melvin looked around the room and not a soul moved. Bradley had been right. There were a very large number of people who were not from Dyersburg in the group. They were mostly from the surrounding cities.

"From this day forward until June first you all are Mutt brothers," Big Brother Skull roared. "Line up from shortest to tallest, Mutts!"

The group began to form two lines from shortest to tallest. The guy nicknamed Light bulb walked over to Skull and whispered something into his ear.

"There has been a correction," Big Brother Skull began. "Everybody who lives in Dyersburg will be under my care. If you don't live in Dyersburg you need to follow Big Brother Rev. Understood, Mutts?"

"Yes sir!" the pledges yelled.

Big Brother Rev led about twenty pledges into a separate room and began a process that seemed worse than the holocaust. At least that was the way Melvin felt. The Rev or Big Brother Rev had recently completed reading *The Diary of Anne Frank* and his imagination, so Melvin quickly discovered, did have a tendency to soar at times.

"Well, Mutts," The Rev began. "Pray the Lord will deliver you from me, The Oppressor. Always remember... I am already a member of this Divine Frat and I could care less if you make it or not. One slip and you are out of here! Now line up from shortest to tallest!"

The group began to line up, obviously not fast enough for "The Oppressor" as The Rev began to curse and swear and scream and soon he walked up into several members' faces and hurled insults at each of them yet no one who lines up on that day faltered.

The Rev looked at the newly formed lined. It obviously satisfied him.

"You need to number off," he said as he looked at the group as if he had a certain disgust and contempt for them. "This number will be your Mutt number for life. Start with the number twenty-two."

The group numbered off while The Rev documented everything possible to document about each person who stood on the line. Fortunately, this process was easy for Melvin and Bradley but the remainder of the month of May certainly would prove to be a challenge and a test. The Rev was indeed as tough as leather and true to his word. He kicked several guys off of line and seemed to have no remorse in the doing. He was determined to prove that his group of Mutts was above average and could out do the Mutts of Skull, Grimlock, or even Petey. He wanted to prove that his Mutts could be the best line of the pledges that had been assembled and designated by city to a particular brother. Pledges in The Rev's group were all from RoEllen, Fairhaven, or Newbern. Pledges in Skulls group were all from Dyersburg. Thos who were in Grimlock's group were all from Haywood County while those in Petey's group were all from Lauderdale County. As the month progressed, The Shaw added a line from Lake County. The pledges from Melvin's group did not know that OPT had obtained a building in Fairhaven and another in Newbern that would house new chapters of OPT. The Rev made certain that the brothers in these remote cities would be able to function efficiently as a fraternity without the help of The Big Six yet could comparably run an organization similar to what had been established in Dyersburg.

To Melvin's surprise, each member of his line was not only an *above average student* scholastically, but most all were also in good standing within the various churches that they also represented. Before the end of May, The Rev had weeded his group down to fifteen. Both Melvin and Bradley had, during this course of screening and pledging, become the leaders of the group.

Melvin's outlook on The Rev began to change as the month of May progressed. The Rev actually wasn't a bad guy at all. He was a type of guy who would execute a plan to the fullest with no exceptions. Melvin had to respect that. The Rev did not care if you were his kin or not... things were done The Rev's way or no way online and within the fraternity... Period! He was easy to reason with yet there was no reasoning with him if he made his mind up in regards to a certain issue. Thus, his mind was clearly made up that the Mutts who would eventually form the Omicron Pi Chapter and the Gamma Upsilon Chapter of The Omega Phi theta High School Fraternity would be perfect or so close to perfect that a person would never be able to distinguish the difference.

And his wish was certainly granted as the end of the month of May slowly ushered to a conclusion.

Hell night was scheduled, as normal for May 31st.

Members of The Omega Phi theta Fraternity assured each candidate that the night indeed be a night of hell.

Sweat poured down Melvin's brow as he ran down a dark street holding the hand of the brother beside him as one solid line formed with the other pledges. Fortunately, Bradley was beside him as the few pledges that had once stood between them had been alleviated from the line earlier during the month. Now, they stood together.

"I'm so tired, Brad, until I don't think I can make it," Melvin whispered as his legs began to wobble and could barely keep the trot that the line had began to make as instructed by The Rev. The march had become long and tedious partially because of the plastic garbage bags that had been placed on each pledge. A single hole had been cut in the top for the head to peek through, two had been cut on the side for the arms to peak through, yet the bottom had been tied to the top of each pledges pants with masking tape. The purpose was to sweat beyond sweat.

"We've come too far to turn around, brother!" Bradley said only in the hearing of The Rev.

"I believe I want you two Mutts to lead us in a song," The Rev laughed wickedly.

"What song do you wish to hear, big Brother Rev?" Bradley yelled.

"Leaning On the Everlasting Arms," The Rev laughed. "Make sure that you link up, Mutts and help your brothers sang!"

The fifteen guys grabbed one another's arms; folded them into each other in order to form what was universally known as the *unbreakable link of brotherhood;* and then they began to sing:

What a fellowship! What a joy Divine!
Leaning on the everlasting arms!
What a blessedness! What a peace is mine!
Leaning on the everlasting arms!

As sweat began to roll down the backs of each of the pledges, an inspiration from within began to swell within their hearts. The louder they began to sing, the more it seemed as if they began to hear the same song being sung in the distance. The more they marched forward, the louder the music became. They soon noticed that the line was being marched toward a particular point where they began to see the pledges from Dyersburg, Haywood County, Lauderdale County, and Lake County. Later, Melvin would discover that it was the ingenuity of The Rev and Skull who masterminded this great feat whereas when the groups met, they sang in a resounding chorus:

Leaning! Leaning!
Safe and secure from all alarm!
Leaning! Leaning!
Leaning on the everlasting arms!

When the chorus came to an end, the groups were directed to link up as one body and sing one more round. When they began to sing this last round, tears began to swell in many eyes as they were directed to march forward again, arm in arm. The music became a thunderous sound as all eyes marched toward a flicker of light in the distance at the end of this long path. When finally they reached the light, Light Bulb stood in front of a long rope that had been extended on the ground.

"Halt!" Light bulb yelled as the line reached the rope.

"Brother Skull, Brother Rev, Brother Grimlock, Brother Petey, and Brother Shaw, what is this?" Light Bulb questioned as he eyed the long line of the group. Skull, Petey, Grimlock, The Shaw and The Rev crossed over the line.

"Honorable brothers of Omega Phi theta," the Rev began in his oratory voice. "I, your humble servant and brother, present to you the Mutts of 1986. Receive ye them!"

"Have all the necessary requirements been met?" Light bulb inquired.

"Honorable brothers of Omega Phi Theta," skull began in his oratory voice. "All requirements have been met according to all of the ordinances of our Great Constitution!"

"By the power vested in me as President of The Zeta Phi Chapter of The Omega Phi Theta Fraternity, the supreme fraternity that shines constant as the Northern Star," Light Bulb orated. "That fraternity that believes in the principles of brotherhood, unity, and loyalty yet understands that quality outweighs quantity, I grant you Mutts from the Line of 1986 Membership into Omega Phi Theta. What say yes?"

The pledges responded loudly: "Omega! Omega! Omega!"

Skull and The Rev went to each of the rope that had been placed before the line and held the rope slightly off of the ground.

"Cross over Mutts into the land of brotherhood and the life of Omega Phi Theta," Light Bulb roared.

One by one, each pledge jumped over the rope.

When the last pledge had jumped across, all of the members of the Omega Phi Theta Fraternity began to sing the fraternity anthem.

Now, the same six guys or The Old Guard as they were often referred who had interrogated and pledged them for a full month suddenly transformed into different people before their eyes. They became nice people. They actually cried with the pledges who cried. They patted everyone on the back and even hugged a few of the new members of the fraternity.

That evening, a huge party was given in honor of the new members. Alumni members and parents were asked to attend a more formal celebration on June 1st. But on May 31st, "Hell Night" was totally dedicated to the pledges who managed to cross over into the ranks of the Omega Phi Theta Fraternity.

"We made it!" Melvin cried after he jumped over the rope.

"Yeah, we made it," Bradley whispered into Melvin's ear. "... Sister!"

Melvin could not help but laugh as tears flowed from his face. He had never felt such exhilaration as he felt at that moment. He was now a member of one of the only prominent organizations for African American high school men - a group that would have positive influences on his life and yet allow his creative ideas to flow. Yes, he had to "lean on the everlasting arms" in order to even make that last mile of the way... but he had accomplished it! He had accomplished it against all odds! He knew that if it were discovered that he was gay, he'd be thrown out on his butt, but he was willing to take the chance and to take the risk just as he had taken a chance to pledge.

On June 1st, a Confirmation Service was held at the Bruce community Center in Dyersburg, Tennessee. As promised, it was a more formal affair. All of the local dignitaries were present as well as all of the parents of the sons who had crossed over. It was on this night that Melvin first heard his father give him encouraging words.

"Son, I'm proud of you." Clarence sated. "I really didn't think you could make it but you proved me wrong indeed. I just wanted you to know how proud I am that you proved me wrong!"

"Thanks, dad," Melvin said as his father gave him the first hug that he could remember since he was six years old.

Melvin received a greater shock when he discovered that the line of 1986 had unanimously elected him President of the Omicron Pi chapter of the Omega Phi Theta Fraternity that would conveniently meet at the James Funeral Home Chapel every Tuesday evening at 7:00 P.M. provided there were no wakes or funerals on that evening. He was also shocked when it was announced that both he and Bradley were elected by the Line of 1986 to serve as Senators from the Omicron Pi Chapter in the Great Council. As Senators, they would serve in the fraternity's General Session which met twice per month in

Dyersburg at the "under construction" lodge hall of the Omega Phi Theta Fraternity.

Chapter Two
Ain't Gonna Be No Stuff Like Dat

Lickety, Splickity, Ickity, Splat!
Somebody's tryin' to get in our frat!
Lickety, Splickity, Ickity, Splat!
It ain't gonna be no stuff like that!
Somebody's tryin' to get in our frat!

Melvin's high school years instantly became a "blast" after he pledged the Omega Phi Theta Fraternity. Any fears that he originally had in regard to the transition from middle school to high school were put to rest because of the relationships and bonds he began to form throughout the summer with his "new brothers." Consequently, Bradley had become notorious in his sexcapades as the two began to grow older.

It was nothing for Melvin to receive a telephone call around ten: thirty or eleven o'clock at night from Bradley declaring a mysterious yet secret conquest that he had with some older man from out of town.

"Boy," Melvin complained. "If you are ever found out by the frat, you'll be ruined." He knew the strict unwritten code of OPT. He did not want to test it nor did he want to see his friend's reputation get ruined at such an early age.

"The only person who knows is you," Bradley defended. "Plus, look whose running the show in Dyersburg."

"What do you mean by that?" Melvin asked.

"Absolutely no one crosses The Rev's path," Bradley said. "And you can't make me believe that he's not gay!"

"I like The Rev with his crazy ass..." Melvin giggled at the thought of The Rev.

"It's not a matter of like or dislike," Bradley went on. "It is a matter of fact that he is gay and yet he is accepted. Everybody call s him eccentric but he is purely and surely gay!"

"Gay or eccentric, the boy knows his shit and if he is gay, he obviously knows how to cover his tracks," Melvin defended. The Rev, over time, had turned out to become the best ally that he and several of the new members of the fraternity had. It seemed that if he suspected that you were gay; he had a particular interest in you and was there for you. He was eccentric, though. He wore a full length Jherri curl that was always meticulously styled and fashioned. Although he was tall and skinny as a rail, he always wore the most stylish clothing to school and away from school. As a matter of fact, he was never caught outside of his home "improperly" dressed even if it was a mere trip to the supermarket. He never wore jeans nor did he ever wear tennis shoes. "What about his fiancé?"

"That dense bitch," Bradley smirked. "Pah leeze!"

"Why does she have to be all that, Bradley?"

"She's just a damned front..." Bradley began to rage.

"There's no used in getting over excited about it," Melvin uttered. "Let's not turn the conversation around anyway! We are talking about you! Who is this new conquest?"

"His name is Jay and he is from Jackson, if you must know," Bradley cackled loudly like a hen in the barn yard.

"How old is he," Melvin questioned.

"He's twenty-two," Bradley answered.

"Only twenty-two," Melvin asked wryly. "Well, the beats the thirty year old from Covington."

"That trick," Bradley snorted. "I don't even want to discuss his sorry, broke ass!"

"Well," Melvin began. "You know that the only thing someone that old would want with a sixteen year old boy is sex"

"Kiss my ass, Melvin!"

"I wouldn't give you the satisfaction of knowing how good I can, honey," Bradley chuckled.

"When is the next frat meeting?" Melvin asked in an attempt to change the subject.

"Tuesday," Bradley answered. "But I don't know if it is in Fairhaven or in Dyersburg?"

"It's in Dyersburg," Melvin said. "We are supposed to wear our dress uniforms. It is supposed to be a state meeting and all senators and so forth are supposed to meet with the head chapter. A Special Sessions of Congress was called. Some new problem has occurred and The Rev has called all eleven chapters in special session this week."

"That means this shit is mandatory," Bradley grumbled.

"Yeah," Melvin said.

"I just can't stand that bitch!" Bradley fumed. "He always knows how to fuck up a wet dream!"

"Well, I hear that the guys in Ripley are out of control," Melvin informed Bradley. "They are thinking about revoking memberships and re-pledging them all."

"Serves those fuckers right," Bradley said as he thought about the constant confrontations that he had with the members from Ripley, Tennessee. "They are always into some silly shit that makes us look bad."

"I do not believe what I'm hearing out of your mouth," Melvin gasped in astonishment.

"Excuse me?" Bradley asked.

"How can you say that," Melvin questioned. "When all you do is go after older men on a daily basis and then all of a sudden you actually care about what the Ripley Chapter does?"

"Child," Bradley laughed. "I'm not going to be like you and wait for some man to come along and sweep me off of my feet when I know that it ain't gonna happen. I'm not giving myself away either. You better believe that I come with a high price!"

"You come with a price?" Melvin was astonished. "So, now you're saying that you're a 'ho?"

"Call me what you want you want, child," Bradley laughed in defense. "All I know is that I'm supplying these guys with what they want and I reap wonderful royalties from not telling. Plus, I like big dick, guhl!"

"You tramp!"

"Whatcha call me?" Bradley began to sing a few bars of the Sat-n-Pepper's latest hit *"Tramp"* jokingly knowing that it would irritate Melvin.

"Well," Melvin said. "I hope that you are using protection. You are aren't you?"

"Hell yeah," Bradley assured Melvin for the one thousandth time. "I plan to be an old, rich bitch with several husbands under my belt, honey."

"You go then," Melvin laughed.

"What time has Broom Hilda called the meeting for on Tuesday?" Bradley asked.

"It's five o'clock at the new Opt Center," Melvin said.

"Are we responsible for the refreshments this time?"

"The Rev said there would be nothing served except water if we wanted to be refreshed."

That bitch," Bradley laughed. "I should have known it. Is he and Sponge going out for cocktails after the meeting?"

"You know them," Melvin laughed. "If things get out of hand, Sponge will get that look in his eyes and then it's on before the meeting is over."

"I wonder if they know that we know that they drink on the quiet?" Bradley chuckled as he thought about the time that he had seen The Rev and Sponge sneak into the liquor store to get their bootlegging alcohol to sell to other unfortunate high school kids who could not afford the risk of getting caught in the liquor store. Actually, had they been caught, both The Rev and sponge would have been put out of the fraternity but they did go to great lengths to keep from being discovered. Bradley didn't have the heart to squeal on them. He knew that when he needed a drink of vaguer, the Rev and

Sponge were the men to go to even though the prices would be ridiculous. Five dollars was the going price for a fifth of *Canadian Mist*; ten dollars for a fifth of *Jack Daniels*; and twenty dollars for a fifth of *Crown Royal*. In selling it to you, The Rev would comment: *"One pays for quality!"*

"He probably doesn't give a shit, knowing him," Melvin laughed. "He would find a way to worm his way out of the charges and crucify the person or persons who dared bring them against him. You saw how he managed to get Spanky thrown out of the frat for battling with him over Dedra."

"The bitch is bad, now" Bradley laughed.

"Aren't you all cousins, Bradley?"

"Yeah, I'm kin to him," Bradley admitted. "But he is still a bitch on wheels."

"Wasn't he responsible for you pledging?" Melvin questioned.

"Yean and I thanked him for it but he's still a bitch from hell," Bradley commented. "He never gave me any special favors while I was on line."

"I can't believe that you are saying that," Melvin said. "Hell, we were the only two on our line that he didn't damn near kill."

"Whatever, guhl," Bradley chuckled. "You sure are defensive when it comes to The Rev. do you have a secret crush on him or something?"

"I wouldn't say all that," Melvin lied.

"I hear has a fierce thang, guhl!" Bradley chuckled.

"Oh," Melvin asked. "Do tell?"

"So you are interested?"

"Well," Melvin chose his words carefully. "I do think that he's cute… I do love the power that he possesses… and…"

"Just face the facts, Melvin," Bradley said. "You want the man and you are too scared and chicken shit to go after him!"

"I'm not like you, Bradley," Melvin commented.

"And what the hell is that supposed to mean, Melvin?" Bradley questioned.

"I just can't approach men like that," Melvin confessed.

"Well," Bradley stated. "I can and I do and it works for me. I was always told that a closed mouth doesn't get fed. Well I gets fed a plenty!"

"I can wait," Melvin said.

"You will be waiting, honey," Bradley giggled. "One day some fine man will trim your tree and you'll be hooked for life."

"Whatever," Melvin laughed. "Are you going to drive or do you want me to?"

"I'll have to ride with you," Bradley said. "Momma has the car for all of this week. That reminds me, I need to know if I can ride to school with you for the rest of this week?"

"Yeah, no problem," Melvin said. He actually loved it when Bradley rode with him to school because they always managed to get into some type of trouble or do something silly.

"You aren't gonna charge me like your idol would, I hope?" Bradley asked.

"No," Melvin said. "Who is my idol?"

"The Rev, honey," Bradley said. "You know he charges folk to ride to school with him in that big assed car that he drives."

"Hell, I can see why." Melvin laughed. "Look at how big that car is that he drives. What do they call it...*The Chocolate Spaceship*?"

"I think his ride is cool, though," Bradley admitted. "His dad gave it to him because his mom didn't want him to have a sports car. So his dad gave him a 1973 Chrysler Newport."

"Well," Melvin laughs. "He wheels the hell out of that big thang too! Have you seen him pull up on the parking lot for school in the morning?"

"I never get there as late as he does," Bradley confessed.

"He rolls across the parking lot every morning around 8:05 on the dot," Melvin explained. "He is always doing about forty-five in the parking lot and always parks in the same parking space. I actually think people are afraid to park in his parking space."

"Probably," Bradley laughed. "With the exception of Grimlock. Now that's my partner there." Grimlock was one of the few fraternity members who could handle The Rev and turn his fury into a hilarious spectacle. Grimlock never would get bent out of shape during one of The Rev's constant explosions yet The Rev never had an explosion on Grimlock. Anyone could see that a bond had developed between the two of them years prior to them becoming fraternity members. Normally, they had opposing views about everything. Grimlock would, being the devil's advocate, do things to set The Rev off and into one of his temper tantrums. Grimlock also had another innate power. He was one of the few people in whom The Rev would accept a challenge of a race. Often, people could see them racing their cars down highway 51 by-pass after school. The Rev would be in his 1973 Chrysler Newport beside Grimlock in his 1972 Volkswagen Beetle. Whenever Grimlock's yellow beetle began to gain on The Rev's Newport, The Rev's brown Newport would always attempt to run Grimlock's beetle off of the road.

"Yeah, Grimlock's cool," Melvin admitted. "I just don't like the way he has a way of getting The Rev started on an hour long discussion, though."

"I sure hope the hell Grimlock don't get him started on Tuesday," Bradley commented. "Because I really don't want to be at the meeting all night long."

"The way I hear," Melvin elaborated. "The Great council will be there. You know that only means that some heavy shit is up and it also means that The Rev will only give opening statements, listen to commentary, and then call for a vote."

"Damn!" Bradley yelled in suspense. "I wonder what is **really** up?"

"I told you the Ripley folk are out of control," Melvin stated. "I was talking to Fred Perry and he told me that they had done something after being warned not to do it."

"Oh hell," Bradley commented with interest. "If The Rev told them not to do something and they did it anyway he's definitely going for the gusto and somebody is getting put out on Tuesday."

"You better believe it," Melvin commented.

"Have you seen Desmond lately?" Bradley asked.

"I see him on occasion in church," Melvin replied. "You know that Desmond goes to Dyer County High School and he's the musician at   St. James C.M.E. Church in Newbern, so, I don't get a chance to see him much beyond fraternity business. Why do you ask?"

"I could have sworn that I saw him in Jackson last night," Bradley said.

"You may have," Melvin commented. "Desmond and Howard Avery are always heading off to some different city."

"Doesn't Howard play for Mt Carmel?" Bradley inquired.

"Yeah," Melvin responded. "He's our youth and young adult choir musician."

"I give him credit," Bradley said. "The boy can play his ass off."

"I think so too," Melvin said. "But they won't let him play a lot of contemporary music."

"Give it time," Bradley remarked. "Mt. Carmel is just slow at certain things and music is one of them."

"Too much time and I'll be gone to college," Melvin said.

"Yeah, yeah, yeah," Bradley chuckled. "Look, I gotta get outta here."

"OK," Melvin said. "You just be ready in the morning or I'ma leave your ass."

"Tramp, I'm always ready," Bradley chuckled. "It's your pretty ass who takes forever fluffing up your make-up and shit in the mornings before we go anywhere."

"I don't have to wear make-up, honey," Melvin teased. "If I recall correctly, it was you who wore it to the last Miss O.P.T. Beauty Pageant."

"And I still didn't get crowned Miss O.P.T.," Bradley gasped. "The bastards!"

Melvin roared in laughter.

"Oh well," Bradley giggled. "Better luck next time!"

"Well," Melvin laughed. "You can't be a damned judge and win the pageant too!"

"Those ugly scanks who ran from Fairview don't look better than me!" Bradley chuckled.

"Well," Melvin commented. "If you told them that, they'd kill you!"

"You know I'm telling the truth," Bradley laughed.

"Child, hang up this phone!

"See you in the morning," Bradley laughed as he hung the telephone up.

Melvin hung up his received. He always loved to talk to Bradley whether it was on the telephone or in person. Although their views often conflicted, Bradley always managed to keep Melvin's spirits uplifted. Who could have guessed that Melvin had a secret crush on The Rev? Only Bradley! It was true, however. The Rev, although he could be a notorious fraternity member, could be a very endearing person. When it came to the fraternity, The Rev could be a tyrant but he had one weakness, he had a conscious. The Rev simply could not wrong another individual without persecuting himself for it at great length. On the other hand, he had no problems crucifying someone if they crossed him or what was considered his realm, which was, of course, the entire Omega Phi theta Fraternity, Inc. that stretched from Dyer County to Gibson County to Crockett County to Haywood County to Hardeman County to Lake County and to Obion County. It was through The Rev's efforts that the fraternity had managed to thrive and broaden its membership throughout the various counties. Dyer County alone hosted three chapters. Hence, it was easy for The Rev to serve as Moderator of the organization. Grimlock served as President of the original Zeta Phi Chapter in Dyersburg and as Vice Moderator of the organization. Nevertheless, it was the Rev who began to become the glue that held the organization together. If there were any problems within any fraternity, somehow, The Rev managed to be in the midst of the solution in order to bring calm and resolution to the organization. His charm and whit made anyone who came in contact with him either immediately love him or immediately despise him. It was somewhat amazing to Melvin to realize that this young man was still in high school!

Tuesday came quicker than Melvin had desired. Information had begun to surface from city to city on why the Great Council of Alumni had been invited to attend a Congress of O.P.T. Normally, the Great Council only served as a figure head that only came to annual events yet never to Congress. When one saw members of the Great Council, however, one could easily understand how The Rev, Grimlock, The Shaw, Petey, Sponge, Smurf, or even D.D. and any of the other members from Dyersburg were as tough as nails. The Great Council had pledged these individuals and although they were alumni, they too had gone on to become successful men in life. Like the Congress, the Council members were all no-nonsense people.

As Melvin and Bradley entered the Hall of Congress in the O.P.T. complex, Melvin was surprised to see that Senators from the various cities were present. Senators from Ripley, Newbern, Fairhaven, Tiptonville, Halls, Alamo, Brownsville, Maury City, Humboldt, Covington, Bolivar, and even Somerville were all there. Bradley was shocked when he noted that the senators from Trenton showed up.

"The Rev must have put the fear of God into these people," Bradley whispered into Melvin's ear as they took their seats in the hall. "Trenton never shows up!"

"I know," Melvin whispered as they found their assigned seats within the Great Hall. The Congressional Hall or the Great Hall as it was often referred was indeed a magnificent room. It was a room shaped like a hexagon and was arranged into an auditorium for meetings such as this. At the front of the room, the speaker's podium stood on a slightly raised platform. This podium was elaborately decorated with the Omega Phi Theta Flag. A huge floral arrangement bearing yellow roses and blue carnations sat on each side of the podium. To the left of the podium, a second raised platform held the desk of the members of the Executive Board of Officers. Each member of the Executive Board was present on this evening. To the right of the podium was a second raised platform which held the desks of the Great Council of Alumni. Usually, this section was seldom filled yet on tonight all of the desks were filled completely. The Congressional desks were arranged in the shape of a giant Omega symbol within the room. Each Senator's name, pledge date, and nickname were placed on the front of his seat in Congress. The walls of the Congressional Hall bore the individual photos of each member of the fraternity with his name, pledge number and year, and years of service beneath it. Behind the podium were two large photos: one bore the photograph of the founding members and the second bore a photograph of "The Big Six of 1985" dressed in tuxedos for the 1985 New Year's Eve Ball.

Melvin exchanged pleasantries and greetings with brothers from around the region before he took his seat. His seat was directly beside Bradley's seat near the front of the assembly. Just as he was about to sit down, The Rev approached the podium.

"This Session of Congress for the Omega Phi theta Fraternity, incorporated is officially open," he announced. "Let us stand for the anthem."

The entire organization stood as Howard Avery began playing *Omega Forever* on the spanking brand new Baldwin piano that had recently been donated.

Melvin sang with as much enthusiasm and vigor as did the other members. When the group began to sing the second verse, Melvin took a long look at Howard. He smiled when he thought about Howard's journey as a pianist. Although Howard was a few years older than he and attended Dyer County high School rather than Dyersburg High School, they still attended Mt. Carmel together. Howard played masterfully when it seemed that just a couple of years prior, he was barely able to play *Nearer My God to Thee* or *Jesus Keep Me Near the Cross* during Sunday School. Yet he kept playing and eventually became good at it. One Sunday, he was offered the position as youth and young adult choir musician after the resignation of the previous musician who moved to the north. Since, he had begun to make his mark and the choir had begun to get better under his direction. Howard was relatively short in stature. He had a huge smile with large dimples to accommodate the big grin. Another accompaniment to the smile was his pretty, white yet straight teeth. His look was distinguished yet his bubbling and boisterous personality somehow betrayed his looks. Howard served as the Assistant musician for the Congress.

Melvin also noticed Frederick Perry, a Senator from Newbern, stared extremely hard at Howard during the entire selection.

When the anthem came to an end, The Dean of Religious Affairs rendered a rather lengthy Invocation. He prayed that God would bless so many people until Melvin knew that even the Lord had begun to tire. After he asked all of these blessings, he began to thank the Lord for any and everything that one could think possible of thanking God for. People actually began to look up under bowed heads when both The Rev and Grimlock unanimously said "Amen!" to which the members of Congress quickly responded "Amen!"

The Rev took the podium again and introduced the members of the Great Council of Alumni. This seemed to take forever which led Melvin to realize that the Executive Board was stalling for some reason or another. When The Rev had introduced the last of the Alumni members, Melvin noticed that Skull entered and silently but quickly made his way to his seat which was located next to The Rev's in the Executive Officers seating. Melvin also noticed that before he sat down, he conveniently passed The Rev's desk and placed a folder on top of it.

The congress applauded the members of The Great Council of Alumni.

The Rev smiled, introduced Light Bulb who now served as Dean of the Great Council, and yielded the floor to him. Hence, Light bulb would preside over the meeting. This made no sense to Melvin.

"Now why on earth would The Rev relinquish his authority to the alumni Association?" Melvin thought to himself.

Light Bulb grinned and, as normal, looked like the Cheshire cat.

"How on earth did this man serve two terms as President of O.P.T. and sit up here and look so silly?" Melvin wondered as he listened to Light Bulb speak. Soon, Melvin realized that Light Bulb was much better at diplomacy than was The Rev. Hence, now it all began to make sense on how he managed to be the only President to serve two terms. First, he was good at diplomacy. Second, he always surrounded himself with a circle of people who knew how to get the job done. During his tenure as President, Grimlock had served as his Vice – President, The Rev had served as his Secretary, Petey had served as his Treasurer, Skull had served as his Pledge Master, and The Shaw had served as his Parliamentarian. In getting to know these sic men, Melvin finally began to understand what an amazing character Light Bulb had actually been in the history of the fraternity. These varying personalities were indeed enough to "do business" and get major feats accomplished.

"Good evening, Gentlemen," Light Bulb greeted.

"Good evening, Mister Chairman," the assembly greeted.

"This evening," Light Bulb began. "We have called you all here because, according to our great Constitution, when it becomes necessary to move officers who are in gross neglect of their duties, we all must meet as one body…"

Gasps were heard around the room when he said this.

"I told you," Bradley whispered to Melvin.

"Hursh!" Melvin whispered back annoyed.

"An application that had the required signatures of Senators requesting it was sent to the Executive Board for the impeachment of the president, vice-president, and treasurer of the Xi Alpha Chapter of the Omega Phi Theta Fraternity..." Light Bulb continued as he looked down at the application that was in his hand.

Moans and groans of shock and intrigue could be heard around the auditorium.

Melvin was floored!

He never imagined that Trent was a "hot spot." He had continuously heard that Ripley was where all of the drama occurred.

"The Executive Board and the Great Council of Alumni have reviewed the application and the request," Light Bulb continued. "Brother Sponge will present the petition to the Congress. Brother Rev will represent the plaintiffs in this matter while Brother Grimlock will represent the defendants. At this time we will recess for five minutes and if I have a motion we will recess whereas two parties in this matter may prepare to be heard during this great session. May I have a motion?"

"So moved," Melvin stated.

"Second the motion," another voice yelled.

"Consider yourselves in recess," Light Bulb said.

Many of the members rushed out of the great hall. Melvin and Bradley followed suit.

"What in the world is going on with Trenton?" Howard Avery immediately asked Melvin as he and Bradley walked into the lobby. Melvin never saw Howard even leave his desk.

"I don't even know, man," Melvin replied honestly.

"It could be," Bradley commented. "They never send representation or funding to anything."

"Well," Howard informed. "I know they did not have a pageant this year and they don't have one scheduled for next year either."

"All I know," Bradley chuckled. "Is that we are in for a treat tonight."

"How so?" Melvin questioned as he noticed how Bradley seemed in glee over a nature that was extremely serious to him the way Melvin saw it, if the officers from Trenton could be impeached, so could the officers from Fairhaven.

"Just look at who they have representing each side," Bradley stated. "The Rev for those in favor of impeachment..."

"And you know how he favors expulsion after impeachment," Howard interjected.

"Yes, he does," Bradley continued. "Then, you have Grimlock, his best friend, representing the accused. They are going to be put out of here so fast until their heads will swim."

"Exactly what are you implying, sir?" a voice startled the small group.

"I'm implying that I would not want to be in their shoes," Bradley said as he looked up into the face of The Rev.

"Why were we not informed of this?" Melvin questioned The Rev.

"You were informed," The Rev commented.

"We were told that this is a mandatory meeting and that's it," Melvin argued.

"That's enough information," The Rev said shortly. "Do you have a problem with that Mr. James?"

Melvin began to fume. As a member of the Council of Presidents, he had been informed about everything else in regards to his peers. Now, when one of his peers was about to be impeached, he heard absolutely nothing. This infuriated him.

"Now, now, Mr. President," the Rev commented. "If the information that I will present to you this evening had been sent out across the board, you and everyone else would have been in greater risk of losing your position."

"Mr. Moderator," Light Bulb smiled and interrupted The Rev slightly tugging his shoulder. "You are needed in the Council Chambers."

"Yeah, yeah, yeah," The Rev commented as he walked away with Light Bulb to the Council Chambers.

"This mess is deep," Howard remarked as The Rev and Light Bulb walked completely out of hearing distance.

"Newbern's files are intact, aren't they, Howard?" Melvin asked.

"Hell, yeah!" Howard replied. "We do everything by the book in Newbern. Even before I became Treasurer, I had the Great Council come in and do an internal audit again before I even began the process of recording figures."

Light Bulb took the podium and then reconvened the meeting.

"Gentlemen," Light Bulb began. "Seldom do we like to enter into private council for such a matter at hand. Yet, it is quite necessary that we enter into this session with an open mind and with forgiving hearts. A vote will be called upon the conclusion of this meeting. After which, the Great council will advise us as to what the appropriate thing to do in the matter and what would be a proper punishment, if any. Please refrain from any further talking among your selves until the end of the session or prepare to be fined. My I have a motion to begin fines at $10.00?"

"So moved," a Senator from Brownsville said.

"Second," a Senator from Tiptonville said.

"The Constitution says that after a motion and second, a motion will carry automatically in regards to matters of the Treasury," Light Bulb reminded the Congress. "Therefore, the motion carries."

The Stated Clerk then read the allegations that were being brought against the defendants. Light Bulb then asked that the plaintiffs enter the Congressional Hall.

The Rev entered with the secretary, chaplain, pledge master, and one Senator from the Trenton membership. They sat at a special table in the center of the room. The table faced the opponents table. As they sat down, the lights dimmed within the building except on the two tables where both groups would sit.

The defendants were then called into the room.

Grimlock entered with the President, Vice-President, and Treasurer of the Trenton membership. They sat at the opposite table.

Sponge then took the podium.

"Mr. President, Mr. Vice-President, and Mr. Treasurer of the Gamma Delta Chapter of the Omega Phi Theta Fraternity of Trenton, Tennessee, you have been accused by the entire Gamma Delta Chapter of wrongful acts within the elected positions. They are:

1. You have not adequately represented Trenton in Congress for three Sessions.
2. You have not submitted the annual fees yet they have been collected by your membership.
3. Monies within the accounts have been spent for the personal use of the president, vice-president, and treasurer.
4. Funding for charitable events and purposes were spent to host Friday night parties.
5. The president and vice-president have recently fathered children.

How do you gentlemen plead?"

"Mr. Speaker," Grimlock said. "My clients wish not to plead at this time until all evidence has been properly reviewed."

A great murmur arose over the assembly.

"There will be order and there will be silence," Light Bulb spoke over the microphone at the podium. "All perpetrators will be instituted fines from this point out. Mr. Parliamentarians, please take your post!"

"Let it be noted," sponge said. "The defendants wish not to plead at this time and by the rules of our great Constitution, they are granted this privilege. The charges have been read, Mr. Plaintiff, will you please present your case."

"Thank you, Mr. Speaker," The Rev began as he stood to his feet. The Rev began to read off endless charges against the accused. Grimlock objected to each charge that The Rev brought forth. By the time The Rev came to a completion of his charges, he had a list of fifty-five discrepancies against the accused. The accused had obviously participated in a racketeering scam for well over a year. The Rev managed to prove how the money had been stolen by comparing receipts that did not match the records that had been sent to Congress. He also produced invitations to private parties. The Rev noted how the Dean of Financial Affairs, Petey, had noted this. It was after he, Skull and The Shaw had traveled to Trenton to investigate did the truth begin to unravel.

Grimlock had gained a motion to dismiss the charge of the two who had been accused of being fathers as speculation until proven by a higher court of law. In the Omega Phi Theta Fraternity, none of its members were allowed to parent any children until after they had graduated high school. If found guilty, a member could not participate in any activities of the organization until after graduation.

Light Bulb finally called a recess. Melvin noted the time was 8:45 P.M. and no one knew if the trial was close to a completion. Melvin did know one thing, however, and that was that he needed some fresh air after hearing about this unfortunate matter.

"I think we should just kick their asses," Howard said as he rushed out the door and into the lobby beside Melvin and Bradley.

"That wouldn't get the money back," Melvin said wryly.

"And to think," Bradley commented. "For the past year, we have had to make up the difference in Trenton's financial loss and they have had the money all along."

"Well, no wonder they never came to Congress," Howard said. "They knew that is their numbers were short they would have to explain it to an angry mob.

"The Rev still haven't given us the actually amount of money these two characters went down with," Bradley stated as he thought about the figures from Fairhaven and how he and Melvin made certain that the money was always accurate. But after serving as president and vice-president since the conception of the Fairhaven chapter, they were not afraid to complain in Dyersburg if they ever felt an injustice. The Rev had proven to be a just Moderator and worked hard to keep $500 scholarships available for two members of each chapter who had the highest G.P.A. and $100 scholarships to the remaining graduating members if there were any. The irony was that he himself had not graduated but this being 1988, was indeed his last year. It would be the year that all of the members of The Old

Guard/Big Six would all move into the classification of Alumni. Light Bulb had already become a member of the Council of Alumni.

The Rev's financial proposal to Congress when he was elected to serve as Moderator was ingenious itself. He did not shirk from working hard; hence, he demanded it of everyone else. Over the years, each event that The Rev had chaired, and he chaired many events over the years that had occurred in Dyersburg, had become more magnificent than the previous one. This made it a hard task for him and it made it even harder for any member to totally hate him yet his mouth made it rather easy to hate him.

Melvin, Bradley, Howard, and Frederick Perry walked outside in order to get true fresh air. They were almost astonished when The Rev walked outside and lit a cigarette.

"Well, fellas," The Rev said as he puffed quickly on the cigarette. "What do you think about what's going on in there?"

"I think we should kick their asses," Howard said frankly.

"How much money did they manage to take from us anyway?" Melvin questioned.

"How long did it take you all to discover what was going on?" Bradley asked.

"Whew," The Rev gasped and began to chuckle slightly. "One question at a time... Let's see... They got away with about fifteen hundred dollars. We found out about it when it first began to happen but we had to build a solid case against them before we can say anything. They were stupid for not making a plea but Grimlock probably advised them not to."

"Well, what is the consequence going to be?" Frederick Perry asked.

"They'll be dismissed," The Rev stated firmly.

"And that's all?" Bradley questioned.

"They'll be handled," The Rev smirked. Melvin knew exactly what that meant. The guys would get beaten up at a time when they think the fraternity has forgotten all about the situation.

"Good," Howard said.

"Unfortunately, that's all of the Trenton's scholarships," The Rev said sadly. "We know that everybody won't be able to afford to go where they want to go while some people can. That is why we instituted the scholarship fund. When ass wipes like this come along and do this, it really pisses me the hell off!"

"It pisses me off too," Howard said. "That's why I want to kick their asses!"

Melvin, Bradley, Frederick, and The Rev all laughed at Howard's remarks.

"Can Mt. Carmel come to Tabernacle on the Second Sunday in October?" The Rev asked Howard. "It is our youth day and we need a guest choir."

"I'll have to check the calendar," Howard said. "Just get me an invitation and I'll let you know something quickly."

Light bulb called the special session back to order. Grimlock gave a closing argument followed by The Rev's closing argument. The Executive Secretary was ordered to pass ballots out to each member present. Light Bulb then read the charges of the accused.

"Are there any comments that you gentlemen wish to make before we proceed?" Light Bulb asked the accused.

To the amazement of everyone, the President from Trenton stood and made a statement.

"I just want to say that I ain't guilty," he began. "If I was, though, it ain't no more than y'all. Y'all are sittin' up here like ya holier than Thou and half of ya in here stealin' just like…"

The room was silent for half a second before Howard sprang from his seat and yelled out, "Kick his ass!"

Chaos entered the room as tempers began to flare.

One member jumped out of his seat and ran to the Trenton President and struck him in the face.

A fight almost ensued.

"Get it quiet!" Skull's voice exploded over the microphone. Skull served in the position of Bailiff during the proceedings. "Make a note that the Senator from Brownsville will be fined $20 for striking the gentleman from Trenton and the Senator from Newbern will be fined $10 for the verbal interruption of the proceedings!"

"Please fill out your ballots," Light Bulb said as order resumed within the room. "The Executive Secretary will tally your decision and Mr. Bailiff will collect them."

Five minutes later, after The Executive Secretary had tallied the votes, he passed the verdict to Light Bulb. Light Bulb instructed the three to stand as a verdict and edict would be issued.

"Gentlemen," Light Bulb said. "The vote by the Congress is a verdict of guilty, henceforth; you are hereby impeached of the offices of President, Vice-President, and Treasurer of the Gamma Delta Chapter of the Omega Phi Theta Fraternity of Trenton, Tennessee."

"Mr. Chairman," The Rev said as he stood up. "I move that the membership of these three people be revoked and that the Walk of Shame be administered immediately."

"Second the motion," Howard roared.

"All in favor," Light Bulb said. "Please rise and take your places for the Walk of Shame!"

Immediately, all members stood and formed two lines that extended to the door. Everyone took one last look at the accused and Grimlock, Petey, and Skull began to escort them out. As they walked down the long line that extended toward the door, each member turned his back whereas when they arrived at the door, all backs were turned from them. Grimlock, Petey and Skull advised them to leave immediately. They left and Grimlock locked the door behind them.

After the three had been escorted out, Light Bulb reconvened the meeting. He delivered a lengthy address on how if a brother is in need, it is important that he express this need within his fraternity whereas his need may be met by his brothers. He then explained the importance of the fund raisers within each chapter and how the fund raisers provided scholarships, trips, and paraphernalia of O.P.T. for each member. He reminded each Senator and President to take advantage of the newly established savings and loans department that had been recently established. After his pep talk, he asked for a motion to adjourn. He received it. The entire assembly rose and a hardy round of *Omega Forever* was sung the by the assembly.

When Melvin and Bradley finally sifted through the crowd and made it outside, Howard approached them.

"I told you they did it," Howard grumbled. "They should've let us kick their asses!"

"It wouldn't have recovered any of the money," Bradley said flatly.

"It would have been a reminder to them not to fuck with us, though," Howard said.

"You are crazy as hell, Howard," Melvin laughed.

"Crazy about money, honey," Howard chuckled. "Hey, Melvin, can I get a ride home? I didn't drive tonight."

"Sure," Melvin said. "You live in Newbern, right?"

"Yeah," Howard said as he, Melvin, and Bradley began to walk toward Melvin's car. "I live on Grayson."

Just as Melvin began to place they key into the keyhole of the car, Frederick Perry ran up to the car.

"Hey, Melvin, can I get a ride home?" Frederick asked almost out of breath.

"Sure," Melvin chuckled. "I guess I'm Jolly Cab tonight."

"Do you need some gas money?" Frederick asked.

"Get on in the damned car, boy," Melvin chuckled. "I'm not The Rev!" Melvin liked Frederick. Frederick was a very attractive guy. In fact, his features almost resembled a woman's. He was a short yet petite young man with thin lips, thick eyebrows and naturally long but wavy hair. He had a peculiar grin when he smiled that naturally warmed the heart. Life had made him independent; hence, he didn't mind carrying his own weight.

"I don't mind giving you gas money," Frederick said as he opened the door of the navy blue Toyota Corolla and jumped into the back seat next to Howard.

"Hell," Bradley laughed as he sat in the front passenger's seat. "I ain't giving Melvin no damned gas money. Shit, this ain't The Rev's Chocolate Spaceship that drinks gas just by looking at it."

"I know that's right," Howard laughed.

"I'm just glad they got rid of those fools before the ball," Frederick said.

"That really did not make sense," Howard said as he began to rub Frederick's leg unbeknown to Melvin. Frederick shifted slightly which made him move in closer to Howard. "I'm just glad that they got rid of them."

"It will probably be a very glamorous ball this year, too," Melvin said with a slight twinkle in is eyes as he thought about how magical the balls could be.

"The Rev is supposed to send us our dress uniforms next week," Howard stated.

"What do you all think about the design?" Frederick asked.

"It looks rather Napoleonic to me," Bradley said as he turned completely around to face Howard. He noticed that Howard had placed his hand completely around Frederick's waist. Frederick's hand was tucked neatly inside of Howard's pants. At this, Bradley turned back around quickly.

Silence prevailed in the car for the remainder of the trip. Bradley turned the radio up loudly when Salt-N-Pepper's *Tramp* came on. Melvin made it to Newbern and turned onto Grayson Street. He noticed that Howard and Frederick began to shift suddenly in their seats. He pulled into Howard's driveway and parked with the engine still running.

"I'm a get out here," Frederick informed Melvin.

"That's fine," Melvin said. "One thing, though..."

"Yeah, what's that?" Howard asked as he began to close the door behind himself and Frederick.

"Next time," Bradley said. "Wait until we get y'all home before you go to playing with Howard's dick, Frederick."

Frederick was shocked as was Melvin. Melvin was not about to say that but was shocked that Bradley had instead.

"Go to hell, Bradley," Howard said as he slammed the car door. He and Frederick went inside of his house and immediately closed the door behind them.

Melvin pulled off quickly. He could not believe what he had just heard. He was amazed that he had not discovered what had recently happened in the back seat of his own car.

"How in the hell did you know what they were doing?" Melvin asked Bradley when finally he collected his wits.

"I turned around and saw them," Bradley admitted. "That's why I turned the radio up when *Tramp* came one because that's exactly what they were acting like. Plus, I don't like for niggahs to act like they can do what they want just because they assume that I am a certain way."

"What way do they assume?" Melvin asked.

"Howard thinks he knows my tea because I saw him somewhere one night," Bradley confessed. "But he only saw me with someone he never saw me in the act of doing anything."

"Thanks for being my friend, Bradley," Melvin said.

"You know those tricks ain't gonna pull nothing over my eyes," Bradley said.

"I see," Melvin laughed as he pulled into Bradley's driveway.

"What the hell is so funny?" Bradley asked as he looked in bewilderment at Melvin.

"Who in the world would have thought that Howard and Frederick would be fucking?" Melvin chuckled.

"Chile, you late!" Bradley said as he opened the door of the car. "They've been fucking for years!"

Once again Melvin was shocked into being speechless.

Bradley had begun to walk away from the car when finally Melvin gained his composure.

"Come back here, hussy!" Melvin yelled as Bradley began to laugh as he returned to the car.

"How did you find this out?" Melvin asked.

"I keep my eyes open," Bradley mused. "Now go home!"

"I'm on my way," Melvin laughed as he backed out of the driveway and drove home to Fairhaven. Melvin never ceased to be amazed at Bradley. Yes, Bradley could be rather outgoing yet he always managed to know the "dirt" on everybody. Consequently, Bradley used gathered information as a defense mechanism against anyone who crossed him. Howard and Frederick were definitely "cool" people but as Bradley had warned Melvin, they too could become dangerous enemies at any given time.

When Melvin arrived home, he greeted his parents and went directly into his bedroom. Just as he began to remove his clothing and prepare to take an evening shower, his telephone rang. He thanked God that his parents had decided to add a private line into his bedroom. They claimed that he was getting too many telephone calls on the main line which prevented them from going about their daily routine and business.

Melvin answered on the second ring as normal.

"Melvin," the slightly baritone voice began. "Whazzup, this is Desmond."

Desmond was a classmate of Melvin's. He was a kind and loveable guy whom Melvin found it hard to get angry with. He was tall yet hefty and had "puppy dog" eyes. Whenever he laughed, it seemed so genuine and jovial that it always seemed as if Christmas was in the air. Desmond had a way of making friend without doing absolutely anything. Whenever he spoke, however, everyone naturally listened because he was one who spoke seldom. He had pledged the fraternity along side of Melvin and Bradley. Because he was always well organized, he was immediately elected as secretary when the Fairhaven branch was formed.

"Oh, what's going on, Desmond?" Melvin asked.

"How did the meeting go?" Desmond questioned.

"It was thick," Melvin said with the anticipation of discussing the meeting with someone other than Bradley or the other guys who were in the car on that evening. Melvin sat down on his bed and began to recount the entire story to Desmond, giving him all of the intricate details of what had happened prior that evening. Desmond laughed at certain intervals when Melvin told him key elements.

As Melvin continued to tell the story, he knew that the exact same thing occurred in cities across West Tennessee. He knew that brothers were on the telephone or in secret meetings discussing the chain of events that had occurred on this night. If monies had been embezzled from any other chapter, tonight had definitely made an example of what happens to offenders. Further, Melvin also knew that if any other chapter was in gross neglect, any funds that had been withdrawn from fraternity accounts got back into the proper places before the "witch hunt" began throughout the fraternal system.

"Do you think the guys were right?" Desmond asked Melvin almost reading his thoughts.

"Right about what?" Melvin asked.

"Right about everyone stealing from the frat treasuries?" Desmond asked.

"Well," Melvin confessed. "I don't know about anybody else's treasury but I do know that ours is intact."

"And you know it," Desmond laughed. Both Melvin and Desmond knew that Desmond kept extremely accurate records. Between the two, there was seldom room for any type of error when it came to the Fairhaven chapter's books. This dignity, they both shared and enjoyed.

"Who are you taking to the ball?" Desmond asked.

"Oh, I don't know," Melvin replied.

"You know The Rev made it perfectly clear that he did not want anybody to come stag," Desmond reminded him.

"Yeah," Melvin commented. "I recall him saying that."

"I haven't found anybody to go with me yet?" Desmond confided.

"I think I'm gonna go ahead and ask LeKeisha to go," Melvin said.

"I figured as much," Desmond commented.

LeKeisha Nelson was Melvin's best female friend. They had known one another since grammar school. LeKeisha was the granddaughter of Fairhaven's first black doctor. The two of them had enjoyed a very special and unique relationship down through the years. They always went to school functions together as a couple. Consequently, they had also always attended fraternity functions together. Most people assumed that eventually, they would marry. LeKeisha, however, had begun to date Joshua Curbie, and unlike Bradley, was quite distraught because of his graduation from high school and scholarship to college.

"Well, Desmond," Melvin said begrudgingly. "I'm gonna have to go. I was actually headed for the shower and then off to bed."

"I understand," Desmond said. "You have a good night."

"You too," Melvin said as he hung up the telephone.

Melvin lifted himself from his now comfortable position on his bed. He picked up his white *Fruit-of-the Loom* underwear, his favorite *Old Navy* t-shirt, and a pair of black, mesh gym shorts that bore the Dyersburg High School Trojans symbol on them. He went into the bathroom that sat directly across the hallway from his bedroom. He locked the door behind himself and began to take off his clothes slowly. He then realized that he had begun to develop his usual nightly erection. He turned the water in the shower on and then sat on the toilet. He satisfies himself, stood up, adjusted the water to a comfortable level within the shower, and then stepped in. he lathered himself, rinsed himself off, and then got out of the shower. He dried himself, put deodorant on underneath his arm pit, and then put the clothes that he had brought into the bathroom on. He placed his dirty clothes in a nearby clothes hamper and then he unlocked the bathroom door, opened it, and returned into his bedroom.

"Good night, baby," his mother said as she quickly ducked her head into his room.

"Good night, mom," he replied lovingly as he began to get into his bed.

"How did your meeting go tonight?" she asked.

"It went all right," he said as he pulled the covers securely over himself.

"Good," she said as she closed the door behind herself as she walked out of the room. Just as Melvin began to settle in his bed and get comfortable, his telephone rang again.

Sometimes this damn telephone seems like Grand Central Station, he thought as he reached for the receiver. *Fortunately I didn't have homework tonight!*

"Hey baby boy," the smooth female voice on the other end of the receiver said after he had answered the telephone.

"Hey, Keisha," he said. "What's going on?"

"Nothing," she said. "I was just calling to find out when you were going to ask me to go to the O.P.T. Ball?"

Melvin laughed. He knew that he was terrible about remembering things that were of great importance to everyone else his age. He knew that he would eventually ask LeKeisha to attend but he always managed to forget. But fortunately, she knew that Melvin would forget, so, she would always call him weeks prior to an event to make certain that he was going to call her.

"You knew you were going to call me," she laughed. "I don't know why I even fool with you, boy!"

"O.K.," Melvin giggled. "I'm sorry, Keisha. I've just been under a lot of stress lately getting prepared for the ball this year."

"I understand," she said. "What are you wearing this year?"

"Well," Melvin explained. "All of the members have to wear our dress uniforms this year."

"Oh my God," she said frantically. "What color are they? I don't know if I'll have time to sew a new dress by then or should I just go and buy one? Lord, the ball is December 31st!"

"The uniforms are navy blue and gold..." Melvin began.

"Well great," she cackled. "I won't have to do anything then. My gown is navy blue velvet trimmed in gold sequin."

"I'm sure that you'll knock them dead as usual!"

"Yeah, right!"

"Are you calling me a liar?"

"Melvin," she said. "You know that the only reason that you ask me to go is because you have felt so sorry for me over the years and you know that I'm one of the few girls who will actually go with you to any of these functions..."

"What are you trying to say, LeKeisha?"

"I'm saying that I know that I may not be no beauty queen and I know that I'm your second choice but I'm fine with that just as long as I get to go..."

"Why do you think you are my second choice?"

"In the past ten events that we've gone to," she explained. "You have never called me and asked me to go."

"I haven't called and asked anyone else either, LeKeisha," Melvin defended.

"Is this what I'm to expect the rest of my life then?" she asked.

"What exactly are you trying to ask me, LeKeisha?" Melvin asked attempting to make sense of what she was saying.

"Am I going to have to ask you to marry me too?" she asked earnestly.

"No," he replied. "I don't plan on getting married."

Silence prevailed.

The storm began.

"So," she began. "I'm good enough for you to sport around to all of these crazy events in high school but there is no chance of you asking me to marry you?"

"If I marry anyone," Melvin stated. "It won't be until after my senior year in college."

"You bastard!" she raged.

"I don't understand you, LeKeisha," Melvin said. "We are not even an official couple. Last I recall; you still had Josh Curbie dust in your eyes. How can you dare ask me about marriage?"

"If we are not a couple," she raged. "Then why on earth do you string me along to everything from homecoming dances to fraternity parties to fraternity balls or anything in the world that requires a couple to attend?"

"Well," Melvin said. "I actually do like your company and I thought that we were friends."

"Melvin," she asked. "Are you gay?"

"Why would it matter if I said yes or no?"

"I just wondered," she said. "Because as much time as we spend together, you have never ever made a pass at me. Everybody who thinks we are a couple tries to come up to me on the sly and then get into my draws behind your back and normally on the first date."

"Well," Melvin stated. "I really never wanted to disrespect you like that but what I want to know is what are you really trying to ask me?"

"I'm not trying to ask you anything, Melvin," she said. "I just want to know if you are gay?"

"Do I have to be gay because I'm not trying to get into your draws?" Melvin questioned.

"No but..."

"No, but you want a dog, that's all," Melvin grumbled. "If I didn't try to respect you and tried to take advantage of you like josh does, then you'd be happy. But I actually try to treat you like a beautiful black sister and then you go and trip. That pisses me off!"

"I just wanted to know if you wanted to take me to the ball, that's all..."

"Yes I do!"

"What time will you pick me up, then?"

"Oh, around nine thirty."

I'll see you then in three weeks," she said. "If we don't talk before then, you have a Merry Christmas and good Christmas break."

"You too," he said and hung the telephone up and went fast and sound asleep.

Chapter Three
Ain't Dat Good News

I got a robe up in dat Kingdom, ain't a dat good new?!
I got a robe up in dat Kingdom, ain't a dat good news?
I'm gonna lay down 'dis world,
I'm gonna shoulder up a my cross!
I'm gonna take it home to my Jesus ain't a dat good news!

December 31, 1987 finally arrived! The members of The Omega Phi Theta Fraternity had anticipated this night for some time because it was the date of the annual New Year's Eve Ball for 1987.

This ball would be the first to be held in the newly built Omega Phi Theta Complex that had been built on donated land located on the corner of Fair Street and Little Chicago Street in Dyersburg, Tennessee. Construction had been completed in time for the previous Session of Congress. Because of the short period in which the organization had to clean, organize, and decorate, The Rev had miraculously pulled together a cleaning crew as well as his favorite decorating crew to begin the process of cleaning and decorating for the Annual Ball.

Chandeliers were gleamed like stars as they hung dimly lit from perfectly polished brass holders. The entrance was lit from the street to the doorway. A lush navy blue carpet extended from the curb where ladies were escorted by their dates out of the cars and into the front of the Complex. Upon arriving at the front door, the couples were announced into the Ball.

Upon entering, the atmosphere seemed magical. The sweet sounds of a sultry jazz tune met each person as they entered the lobby. Pleasantries were exchanged as various people walked from room to room to explore the beauty of the new building. The Presidential suite held photos and memorabilia of all of the presidents who had served the fraternal order and the location from which they served. Refreshments were served in the Wendell Taylor Memorial

Fellowship Hall. This room had been dedicated to Wendell Taylor, a founding member of Omega Phi Theta who had been the first member to die. He had ended the actively festive summer of 1985 when killed in a car accident. Powder rooms had been installed in the Ladies Restroom while extra stalls had been placed in the Men's Restroom. To every one's amazement, a smoke room had been installed at the insistence of The Rev because he was one of the few members who smoked.

Melvin was shocked beyond belief when he picked LeKeisha up for the ball. She was indeed a breath taking beauty. Her velvet gown hugged her shape closely which only revealed her shapely figure eight. The gown was trimmed in gold sequin to reveal a very voluptuous cleavage. To Melvin's amazement, the gown had a train which only added more glamour to her look. He presented her with the normal corsage that he presented her each event ~ a very large yellow chrysanthemum that was trimmed in blue and gold ribbons with the Omega Phi Theta symbols lying directly in the center of the flower.

Melvin had privately thanked God that his father allowed him the opportunity to use one of the company limousines from the funeral home.

"You look stunning," Melvin said as he led LeKeisha to the limousine.

"Thank you," she responded..

"Damn, what happened?" Bradley said as LeKeisha stepped into the limousine. "I believe this is the prettiest that I've ever seen you, LeKeisha!"

"Go to hell, Bradley," LeKeisha responded. "Where's your date anyway?"

"We are on our way to pick her up now," Bradley said evenly.

Melvin drove to Newbern to pick Bradley's date up. Melvin beamed with excitement when Bradley escorted her out of the house. She did not measure up to LeKeisha in any way. She wore a white gown that looked as if it came straight out of the antebellum south. It had an extremely wide hoop skirt which made it slightly difficult for her to get into the vehicle. When she first tried to get into the limousine, her skirts were far too wide for her to enter without first sitting down and then pulling the endless amounts of garment into the vehicle. When finally she managed to get the entire skirt into the car, it flopped up to the ceiling. Melvin laughed slightly.

"Hello," she managed softly trying to hide her irritation with her dress.

"Hi," LeKeisha responded first. "I'm LeKeisha Nelson and it's a pleasure to meet you."

"I'm Adrianne Avery, nice to meet you," the young lady responded as if she didn't care at this point whether or not she was even there.

"Hi, Adrianne," Melvin greeted. "Has Howard already left?"

"He just left about ten minutes before you all pulled up," she said.

When finally the trip began to the Omega Complex, Melvin turned the radio on. Luther Vandross was singing a sweet melody… *If Only For One Night*. The couples seemed to begin to warm to one another. As it turned out, LeKeisha and Adrianna had known one another for years. They were both cheerleaders for Dyer County High School. They began to talk so much until Melvin and Bradley vaguely managed to comment on anything. They actually chatted from Newbern all of the way to the Omega Complex in Dyersburg which left little or no conversation between Melvin and Bradley.

Upon arriving at the Omega Complex, all four passengers in the limousine gasped in awe at the exquisite beauty they be held. The Omega Complex seemed to carry a certain melancholy about it that night that made each participant have the desire to experience the ball all the more. When the limousine stopped in front of the drive, an usher opened the door for LeKeisha and Adrianne. Surprisingly, Adrianne managed to adjust her dress whereas it looked graceful. LeKeisha had no problem. The two ladies waited at the door for Melvin and Bradley who parked the car. Upon arriving to escort the ladies in, Melvin noticed that LeKeisha had a mink stole adjusted around her shoulder to keep the cool night air off of her shoulders while she waited for him.

The door of The Omega Complex swung open and an usher dressed in a black tuxedo with tails asked the couples for their membership cards or invitation tickets.

Bradley presented his tickets to the usher.

"Vice – President Bradley Kelly and Miss Adrianne Howard from the Omicron Pi Chapter of the Omega Phi Theta Fraternity of Fairhaven, Tennessee," a second usher announced.

As Bradley and Adrianne walked into the huge lobby, applause began as other couples began to greet them and exchange pleasantries.

Melvin retrieved his membership card and nervously placed it into the hand of the usher. A second usher retrieved LeKeisha's stole. LeKeisha then lightly placed her small gloved hand into the fold of Melvin's extended arm.

"President Melvin James and Miss LeKeisha Nelson from the Omicron Pi Chapter of The Omega Phi Theta Fraternity of Fairhaven, Tennessee," the usher announced.

The night far exceeded Melvin's expectations as a thunderous round of applause occurred when his name was announced. He and LeKeisha seemed to float through the long receiving line of various members of the fraternal order. Melvin swelled with pride as he ushered LeKeisha through the long line of well wishers and to show her the various halls of the Omega Complex. Finally, after what seemed to be an endless barrage of handshakes and simple formalities, they made their way to the ball room. The sight was too magnificent for words and literally took Melvin's breath away. A discothèque ball hung from the ceiling while a multiplicity of colors swirled around the room which only illuminated the figures that danced on the raised platform which shaped the main ballroom dance floor. The platform had been completely shaped into the Omega Phi Theta symbols. Melvin looked down on the floor underneath him as he stepped out onto the massive dance floor. To his astonishment, the dance floor blinked at random which only made the dancers appear to be electric or robotic.

Melvin and LeKeisha danced for what seemed hours until LeKeisha finally exclaimed that she could go no further. Melvin quickly escorted her to the banquet hall where tables were filled with punch, soda, and water as well as an assortment of richly decorated food. Upon entering the banquet hall, Melvin noticed The Rev.

"Hello Rev," Melvin greeted as a strange and weird sensation began to flow through his own body at the sight of The Rev.

"Hi, Melvin," The Rev replied and added a warm and genuine smile as he looked directly into Melvin's eyes. "Good evening, Miss Howard!"

LeKeisha accepted a glass of punch from The Rev.

Damn, he can be smooth when he wants to be, Melvin thought as he gazed upon The Rev in admiration. Melvin began to glow when he just thought about this man and who he actually was. He had become Melvin's idol. This led to Melvin secretly praying for a moment alone with The Rev but he didn't know how to get rid of LeKeisha.

"If you guys will excuse me," LeKeisha said as she grabbed her purse. "I need to go to the powder room to freshen up a bit."

"O.K." Melvin said as he secretly thanked God for hearing his inward prayer of the heart. "Would you like for me to accompany you?"

"Heavens no," LeKeisha said as she hurriedly marched out of the banquet room.

Melvin thanked God for faith and grace!

"So, Melvin," The Rev asked. "How has it been going in Fairhaven since the last Session of Congress?"

"The same," Melvin said not wanting to discuss fraternity business at the present.

"Oh, yeah," The Rev said as a slightly disturbed expression appeared across his face. "I need for you to sign a few documents while I have you near. You actually forgot them or forgot to sign them at the last Session of Congress."

"Sure," Melvin said happily. He was ecstatic to be able to get away from the ball and get the opportunity to be in the presence of The Rev if for no longer than a brief moment.

"I won't keep you too long from your date," The Rev said as he gently placed a hand on Melvin's shoulder.

This action made Melvin want to melt.

"She'll be fine," Melvin said. "She saw another one of her cheerleader friends on the way to the powder room. You know what that means?"

"Girl talk," The Rev laughed as he led Melvin to his small but ornate office.

Upon entering the office, The Rev headed straight for a file cabinet while Melvin shut and locked the door behind them. The Rev began to search through the file cabinet for the document while Melvin began to admire The Rev' photographs of various events in the fraternity that had been strategically placed around the office.

"Here it is," The Rev said as he retrieved the desired documents. "Just sign them in the appropriate place beside your name."

The Rev sat down in a high chair behind his desk. Melvin walked behind the desk, retrieved an ink pen from within the desk, and gently slid the documents to the corner of the desk where The Rev sat. Melvin's heart began to race because he was standing so close to The Rev that he could smell the cologne and feel the air flow gently from The Rev's nostrils.

The Rev shifted in his seat which caused Melvin to fall into his lap.

The Rev looked deeply into Melvin's eyes. The look was somewhere between passionate yet mysterious. Melvin would later discover in life that this look was considered the "test" of gaydar.

Melvin could not resist.

For a long while now, he had wanted to be in the arms of The Rev and finally opportunity and fate had presented itself. Melvin wanted this to be a night to remember and he dearly aspired to make something special of the moment. He placed his arms around The Rev's broad shoulders and began to passionately kiss him. He prayed that he had not misread expressions on The Rev's face but he could not resist tasting The Rev's lips. He took a chance at being kicked out of the fraternity or even beaten up yet it was a chance that he was willing to endure just for this one moment.

The Rev surprised him and returned the kiss with an even hotter and more passionate, wet and juicy, tongue-to-tongue kiss that lasted for at least five minutes. The Rev stroked Melvin's back with huge and strong arms while Melvin's heart almost exploded with passion.

Suddenly, the Rev pushed him away.

This action unnerved Melvin as he began to release his tight grip from around The Rev' neck.

"Go and lock the door," The rev instructed.

"I locked it when I came in," Melvin panted attempting to catch his breath.

Melvin saw a wicked grin appear on The Rev's face as he noticed The Rev begin to unzip his pants to reveal an enormous member.

Melvin gasped and then took a deep breath. For the first time ever, Melvin did not know if this was what he really wanted or not.

The Rev began to nibble on Melvin's ear.

Melvin's eyes began to roll in his head.

"Do you want it?" The Rev asked.

"Yeah," Melvin whispered.

"Do I want it?" Melvin thought. *"Has this man lost his damned mind? Hell yeah I think I want it.* Melvin examined the throbbing member and his nerves began to leave him. He had never been screwed by anyone yet he had begun to have a wet sensation between his buttocks. At this moment, if he was to give his virginity away, he would want it to be with The Rev.

The Rev began to kiss Melvin. Melvin grabbed the massive organ and began to stroke it. Melvin had never "given anyone head" before but he was compelled to try this new adventure. Yes, he was inexperienced but he felt that he was a quick learner. Melvin broke free of The Rev and went down on The Rev's tool. The Rev began to moan as Melvin began to suck the shaft slowly and then begin a slight rhythm. The Rev grabbed Melvin's head and began to guide him. Soon, The Rev could not control himself and gushed cum completely into Melvin's face.

Eventually, The Rev's panting subsided. He looked into Melvin's face and realized what a mess he had made. He immediately reached into his desk and grabbed a box of tissue. He cleaned Melvin's face.

Melvin did not want The Rev to wipe anything from his face as he wanted wear the evidence of his conquest for the remainder of the ball. He truly was in love with The Rev and dearly hope and prayed The Rev had the same feelings for him. At this moment, Melvin wanted to go further with The Rev.

"We've got to get back," The Rev commented as he placed his organ back inside of his pants and proceeded to zip his pants up.

"Yeah," Melvin said begrudgingly. "I know."

Melvin stood up and then went into The Rev's private restroom. While inside, he grabbed a towel and then washed his face clear of any evidence of what had just occurred.

When he returned, The Rev kissed him again. Melvin slid his hands behind The Rev's head and passionately returned the kiss.

"God, he feels so good," Melvin thought.

The Rev released Melvin's grip and then opened the door of his office, walked down the hallway, and disappeared into the crowded ballroom.

Melvin sat for a more than thirty minutes in The Rev's office alone. He dearly tried to hold on to the moment forever. He began to look around The Rev's office at the various photographs. Whenever he saw one of The Rev, his heart began to ache. Melvin began to fall in love with The Rev's smile beneath his dimples; the way his left eyebrow arched upward with a slight smirk on his face whenever he was about to say something clever; the way he walked with his head upright; and above all the member that protruded between his legs. Melvin wanted this man!

Chapter Four
Faith & Grace Is All I Need

When my burdens are hard to bear
And there's no one to help me share
I just call on King Jesus
I know He'll surely hear!
He took my load away
And that's when I began to say:
"Just a little more faith and grace,
That's all I need!

Graduation from Dyersburg High School finally came to Melvin and Bradley in 1989. One week prior to graduation, however, a custom of the Omega Phi Theta Fraternity was to host its Annual Omega-Omega Ceremony for the graduating brothers. This service always commenced in Dyersburg at the Omega Complex. It was a ceremony to induct members of the fraternal order into the Alumni Association as well as to present each graduate with a scholarship. Down through the years, each chapter had diligently raised money whereas every member would receive a scholarship of no less than $100 yet no more than $500.

Melvin was quite surprised to see so many people in attendance to the 1989 Omega-Omega Ceremony. It was not feasibly possible to have a greater service than the 1988 Omega-Omega Ceremony due to the fact that The Rev, Grimlock, Petey, The Shaw and Skull all celebrated their final year of high school together. They were the last of the Old Guard/Big Six and because of this, the celebration and ceremony lasted for an entire week. Many members cried or declared glorious oaths to the works that had been accomplished because of these brothers.

When fraternity began preparations for the Omega-Omega Ceremonies of The Old Guard/Big Six, the Omega Complex had been decorated from top to bottom in navy blue and gold banners and

Omega Phi theta insignia. Photographs from all events that the five brothers had participated in were hung strategically around the building. Because these brothers were all members of The Old Guard/Big Six, the membership voted to celebrate each ceremony individually in order to reflect the life and service of each member. Therefore, for five days, the Omega complex was filled with well wishers and members.

Petey's Omega-Omega Ceremony opened the weeklong festival. It was held on Monday evening. Petey's Ceremony had been rather quiet and dignified. His mother had chosen Mozart, Bach, and Mendelssohn to be played as the guest arrived. The brothers who pledged Omega Phi Theta under Petey's leadership rendered speeches in his behalf. The assembly applauded the accomplishments of Petey. The Rev presented him with a shield, gold tipped cane, and a plaque. A reception was held in the fellowship hall following the services.

The Shaw's Omega-Omega Ceremony that followed on Tuesday evening had a slightly different twist. At The Shaw's request, there was no long ceremony but a banquet held instead in the fellowship hall. The fraternity obliged him. The Rev presented The Shaw with similar memorabilia that he had presented Petey with and served as the keynote speaker during the banquet. The brothers who pledged Omega Phi Theta under The Shaw were noted for being great "steppers" and presented The Shaw with a step presentation.

On Wednesday evening, no one knew what to expect. The fraternal air had begun to become festive yet everyone knew that the last three Omega-Omega Ceremonies would be held in honor of the last three members of the Old Guard/Big Six. Everyone knew that Skull, Grimlock, and The Rev had contributed greatly to the fraternity yet no one knew what to expect yet everyone knew that the occasions would turn into memorable events.

Skull pulled up to the Omega complex in a navy blue Fleetwood Cadillac followed by an entourage of important fraternity members who also drove Fleetwood Cadillacs. Upon entering the Omega complex, the sounds of Sade could be heard floating through the air. The skull had requested that no one dress in dress uniform for his Omega-Omega Ceremony but to come in casual attire. The membership complied. A lengthy program had been prepared in honor of Skull. Being a sports hero, many of the speakers of the evening were affiliated with sports. Members from the fraternity who pledged under Skull gave lengthy testimonies of how Skull, through his athletic prowess, managed to keep the northern chapters of Omega Phi Theta connected to the southern chapters of Omega Phi Theta. Last, members of The Old Guard/Big Six rendered speeches. At every word spoken by The Rev, Grimlock, Petey, the Shaw, and Light Bulb, Melvin, along with many other members of the fraternity, fought hard to hold back tears. During the speeches of The Big Six, the reality of the ending of an era drew nigh. Skull had worked hard to keep some type of sporting event continual among the various chapters of the fraternity. He encouraged many brothers to become all that they could become athletically but to continue to strive more to become the best academically. He had persuaded many members to remain in the fraternity and not drop out of high school which would have terminated their membership in the fraternity. Though it had been a long evening and program, everyone knew that the last two nights would probably be longer and sadder.

The day of Grimlock's Omega-Omega Ceremony came on Thursday. Sadness began to swell in the pit of Melvin's stomach as he began to think about all of the great times that he had shared with Grimlock.

"Well," Melvin commented to Bradley as he drove to school Thursday morning. "There are only two more to go."

"Yes, Lord," Bradley commented absently. "I'll be glad when it all comes to an end on tomorrow."

Bradley's forthrightness had a tendency of shocking Melvin at times. Melvin was honored to be able to pay tribute and respect to the Old Guard/Big Six for the great accomplishments they had brought to the fraternity. Bradley, in Melvin's opinion, had acted as if the entire episode was some great trial or task.

"They deserve this tribute," Melvin grumbled. "After all, it is a service of honor and they have been the backbone of this fraternity, you know!"

"I never said that they didn't deserve the tribute," Bradley commented as he began to flip through a magazine never looking up at Melvin. "I just stated a fact. I am tired of them. Shit! Tonight and tomorrow night we have to put on that ugly ass blue and gold uniform that The Rev designed specifically for these public functions. Hell, I hate that tired shit. I never did like it either. We all look like generals from Napoleon's army in that shit. I'm just happy that we never had many occasions to wear that ugly crap to."

"You are on the border line of treason," Melvin roared.

"And you have lost your damned mind," Bradley laughed. "I can't believe that you are sitting here getting all worked up and wet around the collar because your precious Rev is getting ready to leave you. I wish he'd go on and give you some dick so you'll be all right!"

"What in the hell are you talking about?" Melvin asked in astonishment.

"You've had a crush on The Rev for years, boy," Bradley stated. "It is so damned obvious too. The sad thing about it all is that he acts like the damned village idiot and has never realized that you want his ass bad."

Melvin was speechless. Bradley had just "read" him! It was not that Bradley had never "read" him before but for the first time in a while, Bradley was ridiculously true.

"Go on," Bradley said as he finally looked up from the magazine at Melvin. "Tell me that I'm lying?"

Melvin said nothing.

"Point taken!" Bradley said as he opened the magazine and began to flip through the pages again.

"The only thing that I am saying, Bradley," Melvin attempted to feebly defend his position. "Is that they deserve this honor and tribute."

"The only thing that I am saying, Melvin" Bradley stated. "Is that I am tired of these long assed programs and I sure as hell don't feel like putting on that hot assed uniform!"

"Oh!" Melvin smirked.

"Furthermore," Bradley continued. "I think the world of both Grimlock and The Rev. I even like Skull, Petey and The Shaw. But y'all act like they are just totally finished with Omega Phi Theta! You know that The Rev would die before he'd take his hand off of the frat. Look at how legislation has changed in Congress recently in favor of the powers of the alumni Association. The closer the Big Six get to Omega-Omega Ceremonies, the more legislation has changed in favor of the Alumni Association members. But, I don't fault them at all because they did build this organization but, hell, we sat right there and voted the shit in and we will probably be long gone before it can ever be changed. Now who really needs to be crying?"

"I never thought about it that way," Melvin said softly.

"Of course you didn't," Bradley chuckled. "You were too busy watching The Rev's every move. I wonder what farce there will actually be tonight and Friday night?"

Melvin's eyes lit up like Christmas trees. He had actually been waiting for an opportunity to tell Bradley the inside gossip that he had heard in regards to Thursday and Friday night's programs.

"Well," Melvin began. "I heard that tonight and tomorrow night after the ceremony there will be a dinner followed by a dance. Now one thing I give both Grimlock and The Rev, they know how to throw a party."

"I wonder what profit they'll make off of them?" Bradley asked wryly.

"There is supposed to be at least four to five hundred people at tonight's gala in honor of Grimlock and anywhere from eight hundred to a thousand people on Friday night," Melvin smiled as he thought about what the program would actually be like if he was seated beside The Rev as his lover. "I wonder if the Rev will cry in public tomorrow night?"

"Why hell no," Bradley laughed. "He will only say that smith men don't cry in public unless it is a funeral of an extremely close loved one."

Melvin laughed along with Bradley at this point. Bradley had a way of imitated The Rev exactly. The more that Melvin thought about it, the more he realized that it was highly probable that The Rev would not cry during the barrage of presentations that would be made.

On Thursday, Melvin decided that he and Bradley would attend the last two Omega-Omega Ceremonies in style. He begged his father to allow him the opportunity to borrow the family business limousine. Fortunately, his father had agreed.

"We might as well not be outdone," Melvin chuckled as he picked Bradley up. "Just because we are from the country doesn't mean that we don't have class too."

"I know that's right, boy," Bradley laughed as he entered the limousine.

"You did bring a change of clothes, didn't you?" Melvin asked.

"Yes, Melvin," Bradley grinned. "I'm not going to forget he after party."

Although Grimlock had been a major player during the split of 1985, his Omega-Omega Ceremony was shorter than expected though immaculately planned. The service reflected his childhood days prior to pledging the fraternity; his years of service in the fraternity; the contributions he gave during his membership; and the loss that the fraternity would suffer upon his Omega-Omega Ceremony. After the services were complete, dinner was served in the banquet hall. A meal of roasted turkey, cornbread dressing, green beans, mashed potatoes and gravy, hot buttered rolls, caramel cake, and iced tea. Immediately following the dinner party, everyone headed to Grimlock's party in his back yard on Custer Street in Dyersburg, Tennessee. Melvin and Bradley were definitely not opposed to this because Grimlock always hosted really great parties.

Melvin and Bradley went to the party and partied with the group until around ten thirty that evening. Grimlock's mother announced the party would end because it was still a school night.

As expected, on Friday, members from chapters from all over West Tennessee descended on the Omega Complex for The Rev's Omega-Omega Ceremony and the announcement of who would become his successor as Moderator. The members of Congress dressed in "state" uniform while the members of each chapter dressed as if they were attending the funeral of The Rev. Everyone knew that The Rev would receive a superb appointment within the Alumni Association as would the other members of The Old Guard/Big Six. Melvin thought about The Rev's tenure as moderator of the organization. In a few short years, he and The Big Six managed to get donors who believed in the cause of Omega Phi Theta enough to not only donate land for the building of a building but supply the funds to build the complex. As The Big Six neared the completion of their tenure as members in high school, they made certain that the strength and duties of the Alumni Association would change. This, like Bradley had forewarned, gave them the right to be active in the affairs of the fraternity for years to come.

The Rev's Omega-Omega Ceremony was, as Melvin had anticipated, a formal affair. Upon arriving, each person was announced and ushered to a seat. A souvenir booklet had been printed with The Rev's photograph and biography within it as well as photographs of The Rev and his times within the fraternity. There was a very lengthy but stately order of service provided within the souvenir booklet. Musicians from Memphis had been hired to come to Dyersburg to play and sing for the occasion. The event was indeed the most spectacular service of all Omega-Omega Ceremonies previously held in the history of Omega Phi Theta.

The Rev marched down the center aisle and took his seat in the front. To Melvin, The Rev actually appeared tired and worn. Melvin actually began to feel sorry for him because The Rev had spent years helping to build this fraternity structure and had ensured that it would become a viable force within the West Tennessee area. Because The Rev's seat as Moderator had been created to be the number one position within the fraternity, many fights had erupted between members who wanted the position until finally the Alumni Association granted The Rev the privilege to choose his successor. In order to keep everyone in suspense, The Rev vowed not to make the announcement until the evening of his Omega-Omega Ceremony when all new appointments and election results would be turned in by the membership. Melvin figured that someone from Dyersburg would actually get the position because Dyersburg was the founding chapter.

The Rev's Omega-Omega Ceremony lasted for two hours and a half. It was the only service where many of the members cried honest tears of sadness at The Rev's departure. It was also the only service where many members cried tears of joy as they were quite happy to see his term come to an end. Bradley, of course, was in the latter group.

"I cannot believe that you are in tears," Melvin whispered to Bradley as he wiped tears from his own eyes as a lady from Memphis sang *Pay Day, some Day"*.

"I'm so happy this bastard is leaving," Bradley said as he wiped tears from his eyes. "I just can't help myself!"

When finally the services came to an end and The Rev had been presented with countless plaques, certificates, and other OPT memorabilia and keep sakes, he stood, thanked the members and guest for attending, and then called for a private intermission with only members of the fraternity. The other guests were asked to move into the dining hall and begin to fellowship as a pertinent meeting was in order.

There was a slight bustle as people began to exit.

The membership sat still and the door was locked behind the last guest.

The Rev took the podium and then began to read the appointments for the incoming session of OPT. He began with reading the election results from each chapter and announced the executive board of each for the incoming year. He then announced the Senators who would serve in Congress for the upcoming Session. He then announced the appointments to the various standing committees. Last, he announced the members of the Executive Council beginning with the least position and completing at the 1st and 2nd Vice – Moderator.

"Now," The Rev said smugly. "The moment you've all been waiting for. By the power vested in me as Moderator of the Omega Phi Theta Fraternity, Incorporated, I nominate as my successor,

Sponge from the Zeta Phi Chapter of The Omega Phi Theta Fraternity in Dyersburg, Tennessee."

Melvin knew that The Rev's successor would be from Dyersburg.

Everyone applauded.

"May I get a motion to elect him?" The Rev asked.

"So moved," Bradley said.

"Second the motion," Howard yelled.

"All in favor," The Rev called. "Say aye!"

"Aye," the membership yelled.

"All opposed say nay," The Rev commented.

The building went silent.

"Well," The Rev said as Sponge approached the podium, "I hereby pass the scepter of The Moderator of the Omega Phi Theta Fraternity, Incorporated into the hands of Sponge."

Sponge received the scepter and the membership applauded.

After The Rev placed the Omegan scepter into Sponge's hand, he waved to the crowd and took a seat amongst the Alumni. Sponge thanked The Rev and the fraternity for choosing him as the successor of an Omegan hero.

Again, the crowd erupted into applause.

"I wish he would shut up and go on and announce the dance so we can get outta here," Bradley grumbled.

"Tonight there will be a slight change in our normal routine," sponge commented. "The Rev has graciously provided us with dinner and dance out on the Lake. Anyone who does not have transportation will need to speak immediately with a representative from the transportation committee. Thank you and good night."

"Who wants to go to the damned Lake?" Bradley fussed.

"You just can't be satisfied, can you?" Melvin asked.

"I don't wanna go to no damned Realfoot Lake with all of those fucking snakes up there," Bradley grumbled.

"Then keep your ass here, then," Melvin retorted as he walked away from Bradley and disappeared into the crowd of well-wishers.

1989 had been a successful school year and it had also been a successful year within the fraternity as well for Melvin. He would graduate within the top ten percent of his class. He had served his fraternity well also. As a Senator in the Omegan Congress, he had made a few noteworthy moves that made him a celebrity. At school, he had also had a few noteworthy accomplishments. Because he had served on the Student council, The National Honors Society, Young Life, The Drama Club, The Debate Team, and was a member of the Track & Field Team, he had been deemed him a celebrity as well. He was pleased at his accomplishments.

Bradley had become a basketball and track star. When Melvin asked him why he chose to play, he replied: "Because I know that I can play basketball and because I wanna be able to see all of that dick, child." Unfortunately, people had begun to suspect that Bradley was either bi-sexual or gay because he would sometimes get careless or "messy" with his business.

During the mid to late 1980's, Dyersburg High School's basketball team played in the state championship tournament every year. The boys' championship playoffs were always held in Nashville, Tennessee while the girls' championship playoffs were always held in Murfreesboro, Tennessee. Normally, Dyersburg would shut down almost completely during this tournament. The city school system would close and charter buses to drive to Nashville for the event.

Because Bradley was on the team, Melvin would drive to Nashville to support him. He always allowed Desmond, Howard, and Frederick to ride with him whereas he would not have to drive alone.

After Dyersburg had won one of the final games, the original plan was for the group to meet at Bradley's hotel room and then go out on the town to see the sights of Nashville.

Upon arriving to Bradley's room, however, the four overheard pants and groans.

"What the hell is going on?" Howard asked as a huge grin appeared on his face.

"You know Bradley," Melvin said nervously as he prayed to God that Bradley was not in the room with another man.

Melvin knocked loudly on the door seven times.

Finally, Bradley yelled "Who is it?"

Howard, Desmond, and Frederick began to laugh when Bradley opened the door just wide enough to peak his head out of the door.

Melvin did not find this hilarious.

"Are you going with us or what?" Melvin questioned.

"Uh, I'm busy right now," Bradley said as he attempted to close the door in Melvin's face.

This action only made Melvin furious but the others found it all the more hilarious.

Melvin swung the door open and stepped inside of the room.

"How dare you!' Melvin said as he barged into the room.

"I didn't say that I wouldn't catch up," Bradley said. "I said that I am busy right now."

Bradley wore only a long t-shirt.

He quickly shut the door behind Melvin leaving Howard, Desmond, and Frederick in the hallway.

As the door closed, a very fine yet older white guy came out of the bathroom with a sheepish grin on his face. He did not have on any clothing except a bath towel.

"Good bye," Melvin said as he began to walk out of the room. When he opened the door, however, Howard, Desmond, and Frederick walked inside of the room.

Melvin felt his knees go weak.

"What's going on, guy?" Howard asked with a wicked grin on his face.

Desmond stood quietly beside the wall.

Frederick stood beside Desmond with a slight smirk on his face.

"I'm busy like I said," Bradley said.

Melvin looked closely at the man and realized who he was. The man had refereed the game. *"Surely this man must be in his late thirties!"* Melvin thought. Melvin became horrified.

"We're outta here," Melvin said as he looked at Bradley with a hurt expression on his face.

Bradley stopped him.

"I'll explain to you later..." Bradley began.

"It's none of my business," Melvin said as he motioned the other guys to leave. "You don't mind fucking up your life and your position in the school, the fraternity, or nothing! Do what you wanna do!"

"Stop!" Howard yelled.

Desmond and Frederick looked at one another and then at Howard as if he had lost his mind.

"Close the door, Fred," Howard instructed.

"Well, I'd like to meet you guys..." the stranger began.

"We don't want to meet you," Melvin said with disdain.

"Well, golly, man, I didn't mean to..." the man continued.

"Just wait in the bathroom for a minute," Bradley instructed the man. "I promise, I won't keep you waiting long. I'll get all of this under control in just a minute."

The man went into the bathroom.

Desmond and Frederick looked at one another and then back to the scene.

"First of all," Bradley said. "This isn't what it looks like."

"Then what the hell is it?" Melvin raged. "You knew we were coming up here after the game. You could have at least waited until after we had left before you invited somebody up here. And of all people, a white man? Come on Bradley!"

"I keep telling you that I'll have to explain this later on," Bradley insisted. "I don't know why you keep putting me in this type of a position anyway, Melvin, especially in front of other frat members!"

"Wait a minute," Howard said. "We already know that you two are gay and have a relationship. We just wanted to see how you would explain the fact that you are cheating."

Melvin and Bradley looked at one another and then at Howard and then back at one another again.

They laughed until tears rolled down each of their faces.

Desmond and Frederick looked at one another and then back again at the new scene before them.

"O.K." Frederick began. "I'm confused now!"

"I'm totally out of this," Desmond commented. "I'm totally out of this!"

"I just want to know what is so funny?" Howard inquired.

"First of all, Howard," Melvin began. "We are **NOT** lovers! We are **BESTFRIENDS**!"

"So you are gay, then?" Howard questioned.

"Do you really want to know the truth?" Bradley asked.

"I asked you didn't I?" Howard responded.

Desmond and Frederick leaned forward in order to hear more. Their eyes widened.

"Yes!" Bradley and Melvin responded simultaneously.

"I knew it!" Frederick yelled.

"Calm down, heffa," Desmond said as he yanked Frederick's sleeve. "It ain't like they are the only gay folks in this room!"

"What?" Melvin asked as he looked at Desmond, Frederick, and Howard.

"Oops," Desmond said as he released Frederick's sleeve.

"Look, you all," Bradley interrupted. "We need to talk about this later tonight. I'm sorry but I presently have some business that I need to take care of. I will meet you all in the lobby in about two hours."

"Indeed we will, honey," Howard said as he led the small procession out of the room closing the door behind them.

Melvin was in absolute shock yet he was still amazingly happy. He had somehow begun to believe that he and Bradley were the only two gay men in the entire West Tennessee region. Now, to discover that members of his own fraternity were gay brought new meaning to the concept of brotherhood. He could not express to anyone the true feelings that he had begun to develop for The Rev since the kiss and episode that he had shared with The Rev more than a year prior. He did not know whether or not Howard, Desmond, or Frederick could be trusted with such secrets. He had known Bradley for so long yet Bradley never knew the whole story behind his feelings for The Rev. Melvin had known Bradley for such a long time and they had been through so much together until Melvin did not know if he wanted to confide in anyone else just yet. Bradley had always warned him that a "pack of sissies" could be deadly. Now, here he was in Nashville, Tennessee with a "pack of sissies" and they were on their way to a restaurant together.

To Melvin's surprise, dinner with Howard, Desmond, and Frederick turned out to be a quite successful venture. As Bradley had foretold, Howard and Frederick had been partners for some time. Desmond, on the other hand, was undecided as to what his sexual orientation was, hence, he declared himself to be bi-sexual.

"I still gets mine," Desmond exclaimed in regards to having sex with women.

"I don't want no fish close to me," Frederick said as he looked into Howard's eyes that, subsequently, turned completely away from him.

"I really don't wish to disclose my position at this present time," Howard said as a wide smile appeared on his face. Howard's smile had become his trademark. In all situations, he smiled. He didn't care if the moment was intense or if it were hilarious or sorrowful, he smiled. His smile was always genuine, however.

"Well," Frederick began. "What do you think that slut is doing up there?"

"First of all," Melvin began in reply. "Bradley is not a slut..."

"Then why the hell is he up there with that white man then?" Frederick asked.

"Well," Melvin retorted. "Then why the hell were you jacking Howard off in my car a while back?"

"Ouch," Desmond yelled as if someone had stuck him with a pin. "Touché!"

"You bitch, "Frederick laughed. "How did you know about that?"

"Come right or don't come at all, honey," Melvin said smugly knowing that this marked the first opportunity that he ever had to "read" anyone else. Melvin actually did like Frederick, however, yet Frederick had a tendency to sometimes come off a bit too gruff and opinionated when he didn't have all of the facts.

"Bradley saw it all," Howard said as a light of recollection seemed to appear on his face. "He certainly did see it all."

"I just hope that he knows what he's doing up there with that white man," Desmond commented as he began to pick over his meal. "You know it is so many crazy white folks out there."

"It's a lot of crazy black folk out there too, you know?" Howard commented.

"I'm sure that he has a reasonable explanation," Melvin assured the group. "He's been under a lot of stress lately since his mother told him that she would not sign a loan for him to go to The Art Institute of Atlanta."

"What is he gonna do then?" Desmond asked earnestly. The entire group knew that Bradley had his heart and mind set on going to The Art Institute of Atlanta in order to become a fashion designer.

This had been his dream for years and he had shared it with all the listened to him.

"I don't know," Melvin explained. "His mother wants him to go to Lane or Tennessee State."

"I just wish that he didn't go white for whatever reasons," Frederick interjected. "Hell, we have problems too but that doesn't mean that we are sleeping with white men in order to solve them."

"I don't have a problem with him sleeping with a white man if that's who he wants to sleep with," Desmond stated which shocked everyone at the table. "I personally feel that's his business."

"Well," Melvin stated firmly. "I personally feel that he should remain with his own color."

"Many people feel that we should not sleep with men but we do," Bradley said as he took a seat at the table and ended the discussion.

"How did you know that we were coming here?" Frederick asked as he rolled his eyes at Bradley.

"I asked myself," Bradley mused as he sat down beside Melvin. "Where in Nashville would four sissies go out to eat? When I figured it out, I had dude drop me off here.

A waiter took his order and then the discussion resumed.

"So," Bradley questioned. "What is it that you four old ladies wanna know about my mystery man?"

"Why white?" Frederick asked. "Can't you find a black man to give it up to?"

"First of all, Fredericka," Bradley began. "I sleep with whom I wish. You certainly do! Secondly, if you just must know, it was a business proposition that I just couldn't refuse. Hell, you'd suck that bastard's dick for a grand too!"

Everyone at the table gasped.

"You slut!" Frederick gurgled when his composure returned.

"Correction," Bradley chuckled as he retrieved the cash and laid ten one hundred dollar bills onto the table. "Slut I am not, whore, by definition, I will accept! Sluts don't get paid, guhl!"

"You are crazy as hell, Bradley," Howard laughed.

"Well," Desmond asked sincerely. "Is it worth it in the end?"

"I now have money enough to get the hell outta Dodge," Bradley said as he scooped his money up. "Fuck it!"

"Is money worth risking everything over?" Melvin asked.

"What the hell am I risking, Melvin?" Bradley asked.

"What if Howard, Frederick, and Desmond had been someone else?" Melvin asked. "How would you have explained it?"

"I would have explained it the same damned way that I just did," Bradley said in an attempt to justify himself. "Hell, they are not somebody else and everybody here knows that I am gay!"

"I ain't gay, honey," Howard chuckled as he twisted around in his seat and snapped his finger.

The group laughed.

"On a serious note, though, Bradley," Howard asked. "What is all of this for anyway?"

"I'm saving money to leave," Bradley said. "I'm tired of this place and if I have to suck a dick for a thousand dollars that makes me a thousand dollars closer to my goal."

"You the man," Howard said. "You do what you have to do. Your secret is safe with us."

"You need faith and grace, honey," Frederick said. "You are living far too fast for your own good."

"I've got as much faith and grace as I need," Bradley stated. "I just need money right now!"

"Well," Desmond asked. "How much have you saved up already?"

"Whit this," Bradley said. "I have over seven thousand dollars."

Once again, everyone at the table gasped.

"Where in the hell are you planning to go?" Howard asked.

"Atlanta," Bradley responded. "I've already paid my deposit and first month's rent on an apartment on Buford Highway. Now all I need is enough to get a car and after tonight, I have enough!"

This time it was Melvin who was shocked. Bradley had not shared all of this information with him. He was slightly offended and a bit hurt. Nevertheless, when Bradley made his mind up on an issue, the issue was settled. He would stop at nothing to do what his mind told him was right.

Melvin's Omega-Omega Ceremony was a simple service. He did not want the pomp and pageantry that the brothers from 1988 had. He actually preferred not to have an Omega-Omega Ceremony yet it was a mandatory event of each member. Plus, during his tenure in OPT, he had not only served as President of one of its chapters, he had also served in the Congress as a Senator throughout his membership.

Melvin was surprised when during the services; The Rev entered the room and sat beside him. Melvin's heart began to race during the entire celebration because his hero was so close to him. He literally could smell The Rev's *Obsession by Calvin Kline* cologne and because of it Melvin felt his own sex began to rise occasionally. Throughout the services, Melvin would occasionally secretly gaze at The Rev out of the corner of his eye and began to adore him all the more. Melvin loved the way The Rev could sit so stoically with an erect head.

"If only we could take this a step further," Melvin thought.

Graduation had a similar effect on Melvin. He was proud that he had graduated in the top percentile of his class. He was proud that his classmates had organized the first black prom that had been held since the days of Bruce High School. He should have been proud that the time had finally come for him to leave Dyer County and move on with life. Bradley certainly was.

He wondered what could possibly occur in his life that would be better than his years in high school.

Chapter Five
I Praise God Through It All

Master the tempest is raging!
The billows are tossing high!
The sky is over shadowed with blackness,
No shelter or help is nigh!
"Carest thou not that we perish?"
"How can Thou lie asleep,
When each moment so madly is threatening
A grave in an angry?"

1990 had been a better year to Melvin than his high school graduation year had been. Not long after his graduation, he had lost his grandmother and Bradley had left town and gone on to Atlanta to make a new life for himself. Melvin had to readjust himself to so much loss at one time. He actually could deal with the death of his grandmother but it was quite hard for him to adjust to the absence of Bradley.

Because elite African American southern tradition insisted, he had enrolled at Lane College in Jackson, Tennessee. He knew that after high school graduation, he was expected to either attend college or enlist in the military and, above all, get a job. His father Clarence James had literally begged him to go to mortuary school in either Nashville or in Kentucky. If for some reason mortuary school was not a choice, Clarence dearly and secretly prayed that Melvin would choose Oakwood College in Huntsville, Alabama to attend school. Oakwood had been Clarence's alma mater. To Clarence's dismay, Melvin had declined all three. His mother, Etta Hanks James, on the other hand, coaxed Melvin in to attending her alma mater, Lane College. Although they did support the state schools of Tennessee, Etta and Clarence alike, had a firm belief that African American children should experience the golden benefits of attending an African American institution of higher learning.

An undecided Melvin read Lane's brochure that stated:

Lane College is located in Northeast Jackson, Tennessee on 15 acres of land. It is one of the oldest historically African American colleges in the nation. Affiliated with the Christian Methodist Episcopal Church, Lane is a private coeducational institution with a legacy of educating young people for more than 115 years...

Melvin could not bring himself to go to Alabama to a Seventh Day Adventist School like Oakwood although, like Lane, it too had a rich African American heritage. His simple reasoning was that he knew and somewhat understood the Christian Methodist Episcopal denomination but he did not have a clue as to what the Seventh Day Adventist would expect of him.

Upon discovering this, Clarence went into a rage.

"You aren't going to college to become a preacher," Clarence raged. "You are going to college to get an education! Oakwood, I have you know, young man, is one of the most prestigious colleges in the South!"

"I'd rather be closer to home, dad," Melvin confessed.

"Well," Clarence rallied on. "Why didn't you just say that rather than insulting a fine college like my alma mater? I had some good times at Oakwood and trust me; you can't help but get a quality education from there!"

"Melvin will get a very good education from Lane too, darling," Etta said as she peeped over the rim of her glasses at her two men. She smiled. They were so much alike until it was quite amusing to her. It was almost as if Clarence had literally spit Melvin out and she had nothing to do with it at all they were so remarkably alike.

When Melvin finally made up his mind which college he would attend and Lane was his choice, Etta quickly telephoned one of her sorors and explained that she was on an urgent mission to get Melvin into school immediately. As a result, the admissions office from Lane sent a representative to the James house to help coax Melvin into the decision of attending Lane.

Melvin fell for the bait and applied to Lane College where he was accepted.

Melvin's freshman year at Lane College was marvelous yet hilarious. Desmond, to Melvin's surprise, had also been accepted to Lane. By grace, they had managed to become dorm mates in Jubilee Hall.

Although they had been former acquaintances, a new friendship ensued.

While at Lane College, Melvin and Desmond met Xavier Thompson and Douglas Anderson. Xavier was a Creole from Baton Rouge, Louisiana while Douglas was from Whitehaven, an old suburb of Memphis, Tennessee. The four of them became friend partially because they immediately introduced themselves as being "gay" to one another. Another thing that helped was that Douglas and Xavier shared a room next door to Melvin and Desmond in Jubilee Hall.

Xavier was "high yellow" but short, standing only five feet one inch. He had dark brown, wavy hair. He had naturally brown eyes that almost seemed mystical against his thick eyebrows and eyelashes. He was confident and felt that because he was attractive, he could always have and obtain anyone in whom he wished. He majored in Music.

Douglas, on the other hand, was a smooth operating hefty kind of guy. Like Desmond, he didn't believe in scandals or participating in scandalous activity. In comparison to the lot that he associated with at Lane, he seemed rather average. He was medium height, standing five feet ten inches. He was stocky and weighed around one hundred and eighty pounds yet he was extremely muscular. He always wore a baseball cap yet, when his ball cap was removed, his haircut was basic with no extras. Douglas majored in Chemistry.

Desmond, like Melvin, majored in Business Administration.

Usually, when you saw one of them, you saw all of them as they could always be seen together on campus. Whether it was attending chapel at St. Paul C.M.E. Church or attending classes in the various buildings, normally, you would see them all together. They all joined the Lane College Concert Choir and it was here that Xavier shined above the rest.

Neither Melvin nor Desmond could be convinced to pledge any of the major fraternities.

"I'm content being an alumni member of Omega," Desmond often told Melvin.

All in all, however, Melvin's first year at Lane became magnificent largely because of his new friendship with Xavier, Desmond, and Douglas. There were times on campus when Xavier would "read" someone for prying into his personal business. This would only cause Melvin, Desmond, and Douglas to roar in laughter at the telling of the story. Strangely enough, nothing major truly occurred at Lane during Melvin's first year there.

The first Sunday in September of every year, Mt. Carmel hosted its Annual Homecoming which always kicked off the Annual Autumn Revival. Being a little home sick, Melvin decided that he wanted to attend. He wanted to attend all the more after Bradley telephoned him and told him that he would be in town for Labor Day Weekend. Melvin decided to invite his friends from Lane to attend the services with him and they would also get the opportunity to meet his best friend.

"I'm not going home for Labor Day," Desmond explained. "So I'm game!"

"I'm definitely not going all the way back to Louisiana for a weekend," Xavier chimed in. "Why don't' we go to the club when we leave church? WE do have the whole weekend?"

"I've never been to a club before," Melvin confessed.

"Chile," Xavier giggled. "You are in college. You simply must come with us!"

"The homecoming is an all day thing," Melvin informed Xavier and Douglas, Desmond already knew this information. "Are you all sure that you all want to put up with us for that long?"

"How many services are they having?" Douglas asked.

"One at eleven in the morning," Melvin explained. "The second one is at three in the afternoon plus we have dinner on the lawn."

"I'll come to the three o'clock service," Douglas said.

"Me too," Xavier agreed. "I'm into the church thing and all but not all day!"

"Mt. Carmel usually gets out pretty early," Desmond commented.

"You all don't attend the same church?" Xavier asked. "I was thinking that it was only one church in Fairhill, Fairfax…"

"Fairhaven, Tramp," Melvin corrected. "I tell you all the time that I'm from Fairhaven and Desmond is from Newbern. He attends St. John Number One Baptist Church."

"Saint John Number One," Xavier questioned. "What kind of name is that? Is there more than one St. John in Newbern?"

"No," Desmond explained. "We are named St. John Baptist Church but they attached Number One to it because our church is in the Mississippi Valley District Association and there is more than one St. John in the Association."

"Whew, Lord," Xavier giggled. "What in the world is a Mississippi Valley District Association?"

"Do you ever go to church, child?" Melvin asked.

Douglas laughed.

"I haven't been in years," Xavier confessed. "I forgot the name of the church that I was baptized at. This will be the first time I have set foot in a church in years. I hope the building doesn't burst into flames when I cross the threshold."

"Well," Melvin teased. "If it does, we have fire insurance."

They all laughed.

"The Mississippi Valley District Association is one of the districts within the National Baptist Convention," Desmond explained. "Both of our churches are members of this district. There are two other St. John Baptist Churches in our district. So, they named us number one!"

"Oh," Xavier said. "I see now. This cuts down on the paper work for the secretary."

They all laughed again. Sometimes Xavier could be hilarious because of his sheer lack of knowledge of facts that were ways of life for both Melvin and Desmond. Douglas, on the other hand, knew about districts within the National Baptist Convention. His great-grandfather had pastored in the Obion River District while his grandmother was once the president of the Whitehaven District Missionary Society. Consequently, Douglas was a member of Olivet Missionary Baptist Church of Memphis, Tennessee.

On Homecoming Sunday morning, Melvin drove to his grandfather Jeremiah's house to take him to Sunday school. Melvin declined staying for Sunday school because he knew that not only did he have guest at his own home but he also knew that he would be actively involved in the services for the remainder of the day. He attempted to make Xavier and Douglas feel as comfortable as possible and prayed that Clarence and Etta would not vehemently object to the two of them not attending Morning Worship Service. Xavier agreed to sing a solo during the afternoon program in exchange for staying at home. Etta agreed. When Melvin drove back home, he decided to call Bradley to see if Bradley had made it home yet.

Bradley's mother had not agreed to Bradley's move to Atlanta, however, she could not force him to remain in Newbern against his will. Unfortunately, this move caused a strain on their relationship.

"What's up?" Melvin asked as Bradley answered the telephone on the second ring. He had made it home!

"Nothing much," Bradley responded. "How is school?"

"School is school," Melvin confessed. "How is Atlanta?"

"Wild as hell," Bradley giggled. Melvin could only imagine Bradley's face as he listened to the glee within his voice. Atlanta had certainly made him happy. "I love every second of it. Child, I wouldn't trade nothing for my journey right now!"

"You are taking care of yourself?" Melvin inquired.

"But of course," Bradley commented. "Now, less of me and more of you, how are things with you?"

"Things with me are fine," Melvin confessed. "How is your love life?"

"Child, please," Bradley chuckled. "You know I don't do the relationship thing!"

"Absolutely no one, Bradley?" Melvin inquired.

"I have a few fuck buddies," Bradley shared. "That's all! Nothing more! Nothing less!"

"Well," Melvin admitted. "You got more than me!"

"Chile, I don't see how with all those fine ass boys at Lane," Bradley chuckled. "You still infatuated with The Rev?"

"Not really," Melvin lied.

"Good," Bradley commented. "You need to move on and experience life…"

"Hey, Bradley," Melvin interrupted. "Would you like to come to homecoming with me today?"

"Sure," Bradley said. "What time does it get kicked off?"

"Eleven o'clock," Melvin informed.

"I'll meet you there," Bradley chuckled.

"Well," Melvin said as he looked at the clock. "I'd better get going and get ready. It's almost ten o'clock."

"See you then," Bradley said as he hung up the telephone.

Melvin pulled up to the picturesque Mt. Carmel Missionary Baptist Church in Fairhaven and his heart swelled with pride. Mt. Carmel stood high on top of a hill, an older red brick building with two gothic styled arches on both sides of the front of the building that lifted high into the sky. In the center of the front of the church was a huge circle that held a marvelous stained glass depiction of Christ. The arched stained glass windows on the sides of the church seemed to sparkle a little brighter as Melvin stepped out of his car wearing his navy blue *Giorgio Armani* suit that his uncle Claiborne had sent him for graduation. Due to the increasing number of people who were arriving, Melvin realized that time was definitely nearing eleven o'clock and services would definitely soon begin. What a fashion show it was. Many of the ladies wore hats... tall hats, wide brimmed hats, hats with flowers completely around them. Hats with ribbons of all shades surrounding them, lace hats... hats, hats, hats, all to accompany the outfits chosen to wear with them. Melvin had almost forgotten that his former pastor, Dr. Seats, had recently passed and the church had elected a new pastor. The Reverend H.K. Garrison had come to Mt. Carmel a single man who was attractive and young. A single minister in the pulpit had seemed to be the trend in Dyer County and for some it sometimes meant trouble. Tabernacle Baptist Church had also elected a single, young, and handsome minister for its pulpit in Dyersburg, Tennessee. Mt. Carmel, however, was proud of its new pastor and constantly acknowledged the fact that its pastor was nothing like Tabernacle's pastor.

In time, Tabernacle's pastor had managed to split its historic congregation as the world watched a war rage between Tabernacle's membership. Members who had been friend for well over five decades suddenly became heated enemies as a result. Mt. Carmel had once been in constant fellowship with Tabernacle but the fellowship had been dissolved. Unfortunately, tension developed between the two congregations.

As Melvin walked up the stairs of Mt. Carmel and into the foyer, he greeted relatives and friends that he had grown up with all of his life. As he entered the church, it seemed as if nothing had changed at all within the year that he had been away from it. An usher clad in a starched white uniform greeted him, passed him a bulletin, and asked whether or not he wished to sit in the sanctuary or in the balcony. He decided to sit in the lower sanctuary whereas he could easily spot Bradley upon Bradley's arrival.

Melvin braced himself for the traditional services that were going to be held at Mt. Carmel. He knew they would be nothing like the services that he attended while in Jackson. In Jackson, he attended Greater St. Luke Missionary Baptist Church. Greater St. Luke had "THE" choir of choirs in Jackson, Tennessee at the time which made people flock to it every Sunday. Melvin knew there would be a huge difference between the two services.

Just as Melvin found a seat in the middle aisle of the sanctuary, Bradley tapped him on his shoulder.

"You know that I don't like sitting in the middle aisle," Bradley said as he pointed to a pew on the right side of the church. "Let's sit over there with the men."

"Cool," Melvin said as he followed Bradley into the "Men's" section of Mt. Carmel. Traditionally, The Mother Board was seated to the left hand side of the sanctuary. This section was turned where it faced the deacon board which was located on the opposite side of the church. Three aisles of pews faced the pulpit and choir loft directly. Elderly ladies who could not sit in the turned pews known as the "Mother Board/Deaconess Corner" filled the first five pews on the left hand side of the church. This section was known as the infamous "Amen" corner. Usually, a group of middle aged and young adult ladies sat in the center aisle. Men of varying ages usually sat in the pews that were located on the right hand side of the sanctuary. Generally, the balcony was filled with teenagers unless a funeral was in tow. The piano sat directly in front of the pulpit on the right hand side in front of the deacon board while the organ sat on the right hand side in front of the mother board. The instruments were turned whereas they faced one another.

Melvin sat down just as the new minister entered the sanctuary from his study. The logistics of the remainder of the sanctuary were such that the pulpit was located in front of the middle of the church with enough room for the communion table and two side desks to be placed in front of it. The choir loft, like the pulpit, was raised but raised two steps higher. A side door led to a short corridor which led to the pastor's study on the right hand side of the building. A second door, which led to yet another corridor, led to the classrooms and dining area of the church located in the rear of the church. Directly behind the choir loft was a baptistery.

As the new minister entered the sanctuary, the deacons stood up, and the minister shook their hands as he proceeded to the pulpit. He wore a long black robe.

"The Lord is in His holy temple," he said. "Let all the earth keep silent before him."

Like clockwork, Melvin's Aunt Lilly Bryant who played the piano and Mrs. Wilma Owens who played the organ, began to play a very loud processional for the choir to march in.

"When He calls me I will answer..." the choir began to sing as they marched down the aisle toward the choir loft. The congregation stood and sang along with the choir as they processioned into the sanctuary. Melvin became quite amused as he watched the choir slowly make their way to the choir loft. For well over forty years these same women had marched into the church's choir loft on first and third Sundays. To Melvin, the Mt. Carmel Senior Choir was worth its weight in gold. Although many of them were now bent over from a lack of calcium in their diets, they seemed to transform into something totally different when they reached the destination of the choir loft. Backs began to straighten and bosoms began to heave up and swell out as they began to sing louder in a full and rich yet harmonious quality that could only be heard at Mt. Carmel.

When the choir completed their hymn, the pastor began the Responsive Reading from the bulletin. The congregation responded with him. He waved his hands at the close of the reading and the congregation sat down.

As the congregation sat, one of the mothers from the Mother Board began to sing *I Woke Up This Morning With My Mind Stayed On Jesus*. The congregation began to loudly sing harmoniously with her. Melvin was shocked that the congregation sang in full harmony. One could actually hear the sopranos and altos from one side of the church and then the tenors and basses from the opposing side as all blended in melodious praise. The sound of shoe heels tapping on wood could be herd keeping the time of the song for the mother. When she came to the final chorus of the song she stood up. The congregation also stood up and completed the last chorus of the song. When the congregation sat back down, a deacon bowed down on his knees and began to pray. "Yes, Lord!" "Pray, brother, pray!" "Help, Lord, Jesus!" "Yes, sir!" could be heard throughout the prayer. When the prayer came to completion, Gramps Jeremiah, Melvin's grandfather, began to sing *"I'll Go! I'll Go! If The Lord Wants Somebody, Here Am I, Oh, Lord, Send Me!"* Melvin had forgotten how well his grandfather's rich baritone could flow throughout Mt. Carmel with little or no effort. When Gramps Jeremiah stood, the congregation stood also. Gramps Jeremiah bowed on his right knee and began to pray as the congregation softly completed the song. He began to pray in what seemed to Melvin like such an assault on God that the entire building seemed to shake in a chorus of "Amens," "Hallelujahs," and "Thank You, Jesus!" Gramps lifted his voice high and then would groan deep and low as he prayed. One mother who sat in the Mother Board began to softly sing *When I Rose This Morning, I Said Thank You Lord* and at the completion of her tune another mother began to softly sing *The Fire Keeps On Burning, I Can't Hold My Peace* and still at the completion of the second mother's tune a third mother began *I Wouldn't Have A Religion, I Couldn't Feel Sometimes.* Melvin became moved into tears as he thought about his grandmother and then noticed his mother who sat in the Mother Corner beside another deaconess wipe tears away from her eyes as well. Melvin could not help but feel warmth in this worship experience. There was nothing like an African American rural worship experience.

"If you shout beside me," Bradley warned in a whisper. "I'll never go to church with you again!"

Melvin smiled as he wiped his remaining tears with his monogrammed handkerchief.

After Gramps Jeremiah finished his prayer, another lady from the Amen corner began to sing what was known as a Dr. Watts entitled *Before This Time Another Year, I May Be Dead and Gone.* The church followed her in call and response fashion.

"I hate hymns," Bradley grinned and sang along with the congregation.

Several ladies who sat in the Mother Board and Amen corner began to shout "Yes, Lord" throughout the singing of this song.

When the Dr. Watt's came to a completion, a deacon stood up and thanked the congregation for participating in the morning devotion. He then directed the congregation to turn their Bibles along with him to I Corinthians the 13th Chapter. He read the Scripture in its entirety and then asked God's blessing for the reading, hearing, and the doers of the Word. After which, he announced the benevolence offering. Aunt Lilly and Mrs. Wilma began to play *You Can't Beat God Giving* as the ushers began to pass gold offering trays down each row of the congregation. A second minister who sat in the pulpit whit the pastor rendered the prayer of thanksgiving for the offering.

The time finally arrived that Melvin had waited for. He had to admit, he had actually missed hearing Mt. Carmel's Senior Adult Choir sing. Melvin, during his stay in Jackson, had visited several churches yet no other Senior Choir could sing quite like Mt. Carmel's. Aunt Lilly and Mrs. Wilma began to bang out a tune on the instruments as the ladies who were clad in white robes with green and blue stoles stood up. Aunt Lilly hit a final chord and the choir began to sing *If It Wasn't For the Lord, What Would I Do?* Several women in the Amen Corner screamed out by the second chorus. When the choir sang *When my life is ended and I must surely die, He will be my gateway to my home on high,* one large lady who sat in the middle aisle threw her hands into the air and screamed, "Yes, Lord! Yes, Lord! Yes, Lord" which only made the choir sing with a greater intensity *Don't you know He's everything to me!* Hence, a lady with an extremely wide brimmed hat that had flowers covering it completely who sat in the amen Corner stood up and screamed "Yeah! He's everything to me!" The pastor and visiting minister stood up as the choir sang.

"Go head and sang, children!" the visiting minister yelled.

When the choir seemed to have finished the song, the pastor grabbed the microphone and began to preach to the congregation.

"When your way gets dark," he moaned. "Ain't it good to know that God is everything to you?"

"Yeah!" the congregation yelled in response.

"The choir said, he's bread in a starving land," the pastor roared. "Do I have a witness?"

"Yes, He is," several people yelled.

"Do you believe," the pastor continued. "That He's water in dry places?"

"Yes, suh," several men from the deacon corner responded.

"Come on and put your hands together and give the Lord some praise up in here today," the pastor instructed.

A thunderous applaud filled the sanctuary. Some people stood up while others waved their hands. The instruments began to play a different tune and a very petite woman began to sing *He's Calling Me* as the choir responded *He's Calling Me*. To this, more members within the congregation stood up as the full, rich, and sultry alto voice flowed from the lady's lips.

Even Melvin found himself standing up and clapping with the congregation when finally he yelled: You better sang, Mrs. Essie!"

The congregation clapped, swayed, wiped tears and handkerchiefs could be seen waving through the air. "*It seems like to me,*" she sang. "*I can hear Jesus calling me... calling me!*" the choir responded.

Pastor Garrison grabbed the microphone again at the completion of song.

"It is getting late in the evening," he groaned.

"Yeah!" the crowd responded.

"And, and, and," he moaned. "The sun is going down in all of our lives."

"Yes it is! Yes it is! Yes it is!" a small woman who sat by Melvin's mother yelled out.

"I just wouldn't die," he continued as he set the microphone back into its receiver and sat down. "Without a God on my side. I believe I'm gonna let that go! Y'all are making me preach!"

"Preach!" several men from the deacon board yelled.

"That's all right!" several ladies in the Amen corner moaned. "Tell it like it is!"

When the congregation settled, the announcement secretary eased her way to a side podium and microphone. Sister Townsend had been the announcement secretary for several decades at Mt. Carmel. She was a short yet robust darker skinned lady who sang in the choir. Her haired was styled in small curls that at a glance reminded a person of Mahalia Jackson during the 1940s.

"Fust of all I'd like to say good moanin' to de chuch," she began. "Ain't God a good God?"

"Amen!" the congregation replied.

"I got a *Thank You* card from the Morgan family thankin' de chuch for suppoat durin dey bereavement." She said as she folded the card and then began to read another announcement. "De Ruth Circle of de Missionary 'ciety will meet in de home of Sister George Ella McWallace on Monday at three o'clock, de Esther Circle will meet in de home of Sister Mae Ruth Nelson on Tuesday at two o'clock, de Lydia Circle will meet in de home of Sister Elnora Simpson on Wednesday at four o'clock and de Mary Magdalena Circle will meet in de home of Sister Beatrice Evans on Thursday at four o'clock. The deacons want everybody to remember the 'sessment for Revival dis week. All of de rest of de 'nouncements can be found in de bulletin. Thank you and have a blessed day in the Lord!"

The pastor thanked her as she walked feebly back to he seat.

Melvin's mother then recognized the visitors who stood, offered their names, church names, and pastors' names, after which, she said:

"Pastor Garrison, my son is home from college and I realize he is not a visitor but I would still like for him to stand."

"First, giving an honor to God who is the head of my life; to the pastor, pulpit guest, officers, members, and visiting friends," Melvin quoted from memory. "It is a blessing to be home and in the House of the Lord one more time. You all pray my strength while I'm at Lane and I will continue to keep you in my prayers."

"We show will, son," Gramps Jeremiah said above other well wishers as Melvin took his seat.

As Etta took her seat, Aunt Lilly and Mrs. Wilma began to play *The Lord Is Blessing Me Right Now* as the tithes and offerings were raised. The members of the congregation marched around the tithing box and placed envelopes that bore Mt. Carmel's insignia on them into the tithing box or they placed money into the gold offering trays that one of the deacons held. When this concluded, Pastor Garrison invited the parishioners to come to the altar for prayer. Members of the congregation surrounded the altar and joined hands. The visiting minister offered a stirring prayer.

After the prayer, Melvin and Bradley went back to their seats.

"Melvin," Bradley whispered as Aunt Lily and Mrs. Wilma softly played *Is Your All On the Altar* while the choir sang in a low monotone.

"What?" Melvin whispered in response.

"Something is up with that preacher," Bradley whispered.

"We are in the House of the Lord, Bradley," Melvin grumbled.

"I don't care if we were around the Throne of God," Bradley whispered. "I'm telling you, something is up with him. Who is he anyway?"

"I believe that he is the guest speaker for the day," Melvin said as he looked into his bulletin to find the name of this man who was curiously looking into their direction. Melvin pointed to the name on the bulletin and showed it to Bradley.

The Reverend William Barnes, Associate Minister of New Hope Baptist Church, Wynn, Arkansas will be the guest speaker for the Annual Homecoming at 3:00 P.M. today. Music will be delivered by the Tabernacle Baptist Church Sanctuary Choir of Dyersburg, TN and Mt. Zion Baptist Church Mass Choir of Halls, TN. Dinner will be served immediately after service today. Everyone is invited to attend.

"Reverend Barnes is his name," Melvin whispered. Melvin looked back up to notice that the man seemed to be staring in their direction specifically at them! Melvin looked away in an attempt to ignore this man. He refused to allow anything or anyone ruin his worship experience on that day.

The congregation stood and sang *Amazing Grace* before Pastor Garrison preached his morning sermon. Melvin began to feel uncomfortable because it seemed that every time that he looked up from his Bible, the minister seemed to be looking either in his direction or straight through him. This was a strange feeling that he did not like, especially while sitting in church. He tried to follow garrison throughout the course of his sermon but he could not. He was relieved when finally the sermon came to an end and "the doors of the church were opened" by Garrison.

The choir began to sing *I'm Coming up On The Rough Side Of The Mountain.*

Both Melvin and Bradley cheered the two soloists. Although the ladies were elderly, their voices rang out full and strongly in second soprano and baritone.

At the completion of the song, the congregation sang *God Be With You* and Pastor Garrison offered the Benediction. Upon the singing of *Amen* both Melvin and Bradley rushed out of the church and into the parking lot in order to talk.

"Who is that man?" Melvin asked.

"Beats me," Bradley replied. "I'm a visitor, this is your church!"

"Well," Melvin laughed. "I praise God through it all!"

"Amen!" Bradley chuckled.

"Are you coming back to hear this character preach this afternoon?" Melvin inquired.

"I guess so," Bradley responded begrudgingly.

"Great!" Melvin said. "I have some friends at the house who I want you to meet. Have you heard from Howard or Frederick?"

"Frederick's around," Bradley commented. "I heard he's working at some nursing home now."

"Why didn't he go to school," Melvin asked.

"Beats me," Bradley said. "All I know is that I got the hell out of Dodge!"

"Well," Melvin continued his questioning. "Where is Howard?"

"Well," Bradley explained. "He comes back here on second Sunday s to play for the young adult choir but I heard that he lives in Memphis with some nigga!"

"Let's not use that word, Bradley!"

"Why not?"

"Because we are already called so many nasty names beside the "N" word!"

"Cool!"

"Are you going to eat here or at home?"

"My mother is cooking a big meal at home," Bradley explained. "So, I'm going home."

"Oh yeah," Melvin said as he remembered the reason why he rushed to get outside besides the present conversation. "We are going to the club tonight in Memphis. Do you want to go with us?"

"Child," Bradley giggled. "Did Jesus hang on the cross for our sins?"

Melvin laughed.

They hugged and then left.

At three o'clock, Melvin, Xavier, and Douglas met Desmond and Bradley at Mt. Carmel for its Annual Homecoming 1990.

Bradley hugged Desmond upon seeing him.

Melvin introduced Xavier and Douglas to Bradley.

To Melvin's surprise, Xavier and Bradley seemed to immediately hit it off.

Bradley didn't know what to make of Douglas just as he really never knew what to make of Desmond yet they both seemed to be good people. *They would actually make a nice couple*, Bradley thought.

The group stood outside and talked for at least thirty minutes before entering the church.

"Melvin," Bradley questioned. "Did you tell them about the minister?"

"What about him?" Xavier asked with bright eyes of anticipation of hearing some juicy gossip.

"He's trade," Bradley said.

"Oh," both Douglas and Desmond laughed in unison.

"Now you don't know that," Melvin said. "Even though he did stare at us throughout the whole service this morning."

"That could be good or bad," Xavier said. "He could be a pulpit fag basher for all you know."

"I'll faint if he is," Melvin admitted.

"I won't faint but I will leave," Xavier said shortly.

"Me too," Bradley agreed.

The group went into the church and thoroughly enjoyed the Homecoming Service. Xavier had surprised the group when he sang, at Etta's request, *Because He Lives*. Melvin knew that Xavier could sing but he didn't know that Xavier could "tear a church up" because that was exactly what he did on that afternoon. The congregation responded to him in the same manner as they had responded to Miss Essie earlier that day. The Reverend William Barnes actually preached a very good and inspiring sermon. Like any other African American Southern, rural preacher, Barnes had what was known as the "Baptist hum" which he used to close his sermon. Fortunately, he did bring three strong points that made sense before he took the congregation to judgment hall to judgment hall. Barnes made sense before Christ was whipped all night long. Barnes made sense before Christ drug an old rugged cross up a hill called Calvary. Barnes made sense before the Roman soldier pierce Christ in the side and then he hung his head and died. Barnes made sense before they placed Christ in Joseph's borrowed tomb. Barnes made sense before early, early, early on Sunday morning Christ got up with all power in His hands that we all might have a right to the Tree of Life.

After the services were over, Xavier decided to go to the roster and shake the hand of this phenomenal speaker.

"You preached a wonderful sermon this afternoon," Xavier said as he extended his hand out to the preacher to shake it.

"Thank you," Barnes said as he held onto Xavier's hand and slight stroked it within his grip. "You sang great too. What is your name, brother?"

"Xavier," Xavier replied nervously. "Xavier Thompson, ah Reverend, ah…"

"Reverend Barnes," Barnes grinned. "Reverend William Barnes!"

Reverend William Barnes did not realize that Xavier had begun to slightly struggle to release his hand from the grip that Barnes had placed on it. When finally his hand was freed from this tall, dark, handsome young man who stood before him who just happened to be a preacher, Barnes gave him a business card.

"On the back is my hotel number," Barnes whispered exclusively to Xavier. "Give me a call in about an hour."

"You got it," Xavier smiled as he walked away triumphantly. Immediately, he walked outside in search of his friends. He found them huddled together near the cemetery that was located beside the cemetery.

"You were right, Bradley," Xavier said as he held the business card up as if it were a trophy.

"Are you gonna call him?" Douglas asked.

"If God give me strength to use my fingers to dial the numbers," Xavier laughed. "I surely will!"

"Well, bless God," Melvin smirked.

"Honey," Bradley laughed. "I just praise God through it all!"

Everyone in the group laughed.

Chapter Six
It Was On

Keep my heart and keep my hand,
Keep my soul I pray!
Keep my tongue to speak Thy praise,
Keep me all the way!

Melvin did not expect Xavier and the Reverend William Barnes to hit it off so soon and he certainly did not expect them to meet on that day… but they did! Desmond, Douglas, Bradley and Xavier had all hung out at Melvin's house after the Homecoming Services at Mt. Carmel.

Because Melvin's bedroom had a bed, telephone, and television in it, the group had congregated in his bedroom whereas they would not disturb the James family too much. Xavier secretly decided to stall for time until he felt it was an appropriate time to call Barnes. At seven o'clock when the decision to begin to prepare to make the journey to Memphis to go out came, Xavier finally could hold his peace no longer.

"Give me that telephone," Xavier instructed Melvin. Douglas, Desmond, and Bradley all looked on while he frantically dialed the numbers on the back of the business card that Barnes had given him earlier.

"Hello," the deep voice answered on the second ring.

"Hi," Xavier said and immediately began to lose his brave façade. "This is Xavier!"

"I've been waiting on your call," William said in a smooth yet sexy low voice. "For a minute I thought you were not going to call."

"I always keep my promises," Xavier said and looked into the raised eyebrows of Melvin, Desmond, Douglas, and Bradley who had become as quiet as church mice as they looked into Xavier's mouth in an attempt to hang on to his every word.

"What are you doing?" William asked Xavier.

"Well," Xavier said. "I'm at a friend's house and we are getting ready to go out in Memphis."

"Well," William said. "I have got to drive through Memphis tonight. Would you like to ride with me?"

"You'd bet I'd like to ride you," Xavier said without thinking.

Melvin, Desmond, Bradley and Douglas gasped.

"Excuse me?" William questioned.

"I mean, ah," Xavier corrected himself. "Yes, I'd love to ride with you!"

"I'm at the Comfort Inn in Dyersburg," William explained. "I am going to check out in about an hour or so or in the morning. Can you meet me there?"

"I'm on my way right now," Xavier exclaimed as sweat began to form on his brow.

He hung up the telephone receiver and began to frantically search for his clothes to put into his luggage.

"What are you doing?" Melvin asked in genuine concern.

"I, dear Melvin," Xavier said. "Am going to meet the Reverend William Barnes!"

"Well I bless God!" Bradley laughed.

"You don't know him, child," Melvin began to chastise.

"Melvin," Xavier said as he placed the last of his clothing into his suitcase. "I will know him after tonight!"

"Well I bless God!" Bradley chuckled again.

"You are just loving this aren't you, Bradley?" Desmond questioned Bradley and smiled as he thought about all of the things that Bradley had done since their acquaintance and friendship had begun. Over the course of the few years that Desmond and Bradley had associated, Bradley did not shrink from meeting a new man.

"I love every second of it, child," Bradley laughed. "This is the first time that we've been together when I'm not considered the slut for going after what I want!"

"They considered you a slut, Bradley?" Xavier asked.

"They wanted too," Bradley laughed. "But I always had to correct the, I ain't no slut, I'm a 'ho. I gets my coins!"

"You go, bitch!" Douglas laughed and hi-fived Bradley.

Bradley drove Xavier to the Comfort Inn in Dyersburg, Tennessee and Xavier met William as requested.

Xavier did not make it to the club in Memphis as he remained in Dyersburg that night. William drove Xavier back to Jackson the next day.

Douglas met Xavier in his dorm room at Lane.

"I thought you were coming out last night?" Douglas asked. "We really did have a good time and wanted you to be with us!"

"Douglas, honey," Xavier said. "I did **not** want to be with you all last night! It's not that I don't love you guys and all but child, child, child!"

"He must've been really good," Douglas laughed slightly.

"I read a poem once that describes every emotion that I felt last night," Xavier declared.

"What was the name of it?" Douglas asked in great anticipation of Xavier's answer. "And, who was it by?"

"It's a poem by this new poet out of Ripley," Xavier said as he went to his desk and retrieved a small gray booklet. He passed the booklet on to Douglas. "Her name is Iasia Raison."

"O.K." Douglas commented as he looked at the little worn booklet. "What's this?"

"That is *Poetry by Iasia Raison* in her earlier days," Xavier exclaimed. "Check out the poem, *It Was On*. That describes what happened and how I felt last night with William!"

"Oh, William is it?" Douglas commented. "So we are on a first name basis without the formalities?"

"He's only twenty-five, Douglas," Xavier commented. "I'm only twenty, so what's the big deal?"

"Well," Douglas chuckled. "You go!"

"I praise God through it all," Xavier laughed and headed for the door.

"Where are you going? Douglas asked as Xavier began to leave the room.

"William and I have a date in about two hours in Memphis," Xavier said as he adjusted his clothes and took one last look at his appearance in a mirror beside the bed. "I'm heading to Memphis!"

"This is serious then," Douglas asked. "Isn't it?"

"Douglas," Xavier smiled. "This is the first time in my life that I have ever felt like this! Read the poem, it explains everything!"

"It must've really been on then," Douglas commented.

"It was," Xavier said as he grabbed a small travel bag and began to leave the room. "I've gotta go!"

Douglas was perplexed by this sudden change in Xavier. Xavier was the type who never fell in love but always fell in lust. However, he seemed different with William. It was interesting to Douglas that someone had smitten him so quickly. It was even stranger to Douglas that the person in whom Xavier was smitten by was a minister of the Gospel. *What on earth is the world coming too?* Douglas thought. Douglas had for years witnessed African American ministers totally degrade homosexuals from the pulpit. He knew how ministers, in preaching the undefiled Gospel, would blast a known homosexual during a sermon and make him feel like dirt amongst his own people. Hence, it was strange to know that someone from the ministerial society would dare cross the line and commit this "evil" that seemed to torment Douglas daily. As Douglas began to grow older, his personal belief in God had begun to grow stronger yet his faith in organized religion had begun to quickly fade away.

This man, a preacher, was in pursuit of one of his friends. Douglas's mind was in conflict because the man could preach well yet from his own church; he had always been taught that *God created Adam and Eve not Adam and Steve*. From the same breath of one of those great ministers that would make such a comment, they would then dare to say such foolishness as *God created the world and everything in it*. So, in Douglas's mind, there was conflict because either God created Adam and Eve as well as Adam and Steve or He did not! If God did not create everyone which included Adam, Eve, and Steve, then that really gave conflict to the entire creation story of who God really was. At this moment, Douglas began to re-evaluate his thoughts on the teachings of his childhood.

So many times Douglas had heard since the time that he had accepted Christ in his life when he was seven:

Homosexuality is an abomination in the sight of God. A man will surely die and go straight to hell if he is caught even thinking about another man in a sexual way. Homosexuality was a true trick of the enemy! If God had intended for man to lie with another man then God would have never created a woman. If a man is caught in the act of this vile thing, he should surely be put to death! Homosexuals have no place in the Kingdom of God... Ever! Homosexuality is unnatural and a good Christian should never have these thoughts and remain in fellowship with other Christians.

In conflict, Douglas had also heard:

God is the God of forgiveness! Grace is big enough for everyone because God so loved the world that He gave His only begotten Son that whosoever believes on Him will not perish but have everlasting life! There is no sin too great that God is not faithful to forgive!

The conflict within Douglas was so great on this day that he decided that, although he loved God, he would not attend church or participate in organized religion again except for mandatory chapel services at Lane.

Douglas picked up the little gray book entitled *AfroDeesiAck – Poems by Iasia Raison* and began to read it. As he read the poems, he became enthralled by the poet. He found the poem that Xavier had told him about. *It Was On* described the events that took place in the author's life one night and she expressed it in a poem the following day. The feelings must have been great because Douglas thought about the expression on Xavier's face when he left the dorm room. Douglas reached into his small refrigerator and pulled out a *Coca-Cola*, sat on his bed, opened the book, and began to read…

It Was On

From my spine
to my feet
back to my knees
and near my thighs
behind my ear
behind my neck
and back to my chest
to my lips
to my tongue
to my heart
and its beat
you
and me
simply meant
it was on!

From the kitchen table
to the floor
on the couch
to the door
behind the door
and every room after that

you
and me
simply meant
it was on!

debussy
bach
tony
toni
toné
isleys
o'jays
levert
sweat
gill
you
and me
simply meant
it was on!

Ice cubes
100 degrees
no air
no phone
nobody in the place
and cherry flavored Jello-O
(and there's always room

for Jello-O)
you
and me
simply meant
it was on!

And after that
you ask me:
"Was it good
for you?"

Douglas laughed although he was afraid Xavier was headed for heartbreak!

Chapter Seven

Trouble In My Way

On Jordan's stormy banks I stand,
And cast a wishful eye
To Canaan's fair and happy land,
Where my possessions lie.

After waiting until nine-thirty for Xavier to call them, Melvin, Bradley, Douglas and Desmond decided to go to Memphis to the club without him. While they waited, Melvin decided to telephone Frederick and invite him. Frederick accepted.

This was a new experience to Melvin. He had never gone to any club although he was a freshman in college. He had only attended a few fraternity parties or house parties while on campus at Lane, yet never had he attended a club. He soon discovered that not only would they be going to a club but they would be going to a "gay" club!

"Have any of you been to the club yet?" Frederick asked as he entered Douglas's navy blue 1982 Buick Ninety-eight that had been cleaned and shined to spotless perfection. Privately, everyone thanked God that Douglas had decided to drive. Douglas's car was huge and spacious which afforded everyone in the group a comfortable ride to Memphis. When asked why he drove such a big car, Douglas sheepishly replied: *Because I love car sex and you can't do it all that good in a little car!*

"Yeah," Douglas laughed. "I'm from Memphis!"

"Hursh!" Frederick chuckled. "Then it's on!"

Melvin and Desmond remained silent.

"I haven't been to the club in Memphis yet," Bradley commented for the sake of making conversation. "But I go out all of the time in Atlanta." Everyone knew that there had always been a weird strain on Bradley and Frederick's relationship. To the eyes of onlookers, they seemed only to be able to take one another in doses. The fact was not that they did not like one another but they loved to argue with one another. It was something about the intensity and subject matter of their arguments that made it seem as if they did not like one another.

"Ooo," Frederick exclaimed. "I hear the clubs in Atlanta are fierce, child. Have you been to *Loretta's*?"

Frederick withdrew a compact from what appeared to be a small pouch or purse. He quickly applied make-up to his face and then returned the compact to the pouch/purse.

Melvin and Desmond looked at Frederick and then back at one another in astonishment.

"The clubs are wonderful in Atlanta," Bradley bragged as he thought about his adventures in Atlanta. "Yes, I've been to *Loretta's* but I hear they are opening this new one called *Bull Dogs*. Child, you've gotta come down and let's do the damn thing sometimes."

"I will take you up on that offer, Bradley," Frederick chuckled as he reached into his pouch/purse; withdrew an eyeliner pencil; and applied the eyeliner to his eyes.

"When did you start wearing make-up, Frederick?" Melvin finally managed to ask Frederick after he finally gained his composure from the original shock of watching Frederick.

"After my first trip to *The Apartment Club*," Frederick chuckled. "Those guhls really made me look like I was a plane Jane and I wasn't having it!"

"Oh," Desmond commented. "Is that the name of the club we are going to tonight, *The Apartment Club*?"

"Yeah," Douglas laughed. "I'm gonna tell you now, though, *The Apartment Club* will unnerve you on your first trip but it gets better after your second time around."

"It's an experience," Frederick giggled. "That's for sure. Anything or anyone you want, you can find in *The Apartment Club*."

Melvin still could not fathom Frederick. Melvin could not believe that literally right before his eyes, Frederick had begun to change. He realized that by the end of their senior year in high school, Frederick seemed very different but Melvin did not know if he was willing to deal with this great change and transformation. For Melvin, growing up in the rural South a young, black, gay man was hard enough. Now, right before his very eyes, his friend was beginning to transform into what society had labeled as a he/she, a faggot, a punk, or a sissy. Melvin hated those stereotypes and was very unsettled on men who carried themselves in such a manner. Now, one of his dear friends was turning into the stereotypical type of gay man that Melvin had joined with others to ridicule, joke about, and on occasion, laugh at. To add insult to injury, Melvin had also noticed how Frederick's style of wardrobe had begun to change since high school graduation. On this very night, Frederick's slacks were so tight until they actually gave him girlish looking hips. Melvin never noticed Frederick's feminine shape until Frederick had accentuated it with his style of dress. Because Frederick was short and petite, he almost looked like a girl in the pants. Melvin understood the Cuban heels that Frederick wore because they only gave him height yet he could not understand Frederick's multicolor low cut shirt that almost looked like a blouse. Even worse, Frederick's hair was now a permed pile of curls that cascaded on top of his head into a bouffant.

"Is it an experience that will transform you into a woman?" Melvin questioned as he looked directly at the seemingly "new" Frederick.

"I don't feel that Frederick is transforming," Bradley defended. "He's just merely being expressive of his true and innermost self."

"Oh," Melvin asked sarcastically. "So you transform in Atlanta too?"

"Don't come for me, bitch," Bradley said shortly. "You know I'll eat your ass alive, guhl!"

"Does this *Apartment Club* transform you into a fully fledged woman?" Melvin asked. "If so, I don't want to go!"

"What the hell does that mean?" Frederick asked.

"You look like you are turning into some faggot bitch," Melvin replied shortly.

Bradley, Frederick, Douglas, and Desmond's eyes widened.

"Y'all are so damned country and silly," Bradley said quickly in order to diffuse a situation within the car. "If Frederick wants to get in touch with his feminine side, how does that bother you saints?"

"I just feel that men should..." Melvin began.

"You just feel what?" Frederick said hotly. "you haven't even been fucked yet, bitch, and now you want to be some God damned authority on how a person should feel! Bitch shut the hell up! I'm so sick and tired of having to live up to other mothafucka's standards until I could just scream. Bitch, just shut up!"

Frederick's words stung but Melvin could definitely relate.

"Now, now, guhls, let's not throw daggers tonight," Bradley interjected in an attempt to diffuse a possible atomic bomb being lowered into the car. Bradley had witnessed far too many battles between gay men in Atlanta. He was just not up to it on this night. He, like everyone else, just wanted to have a good time with friends before he returned back to Atlanta.

"I'm not throwing daggers," Frederick commented as he retrieved his compact from his pouch/purse and began to apply another layer of make-up to his face. "But I will not sit here and listen to a lot of shit from somebody who is afraid to be gay!"

"I just feel..." Melvin began.

"Didn't I tell your silly ass that I don't give a sweet fuck what you feel?" Frederick questioned. "Here, maybe you need to try a little of my foundation! Maybe you will get laid for the first time in your life by trying something new!"

"How do you know if I have or have not been laid yet?" Melvin asked Frederick.

"Correct me if I'm wrong," Frederick said. "But you are the bitch who no less than an hour ago made the glorious declaration that you are still a vestal virgin and nobody has every tapped those cookies before!"

Bradley roared in laughter.

"You two are tripping," Desmond responded as he joined Bradley's laughter.

"They sure are," Douglas laughed. "Hell, we are all gay! The best part about being gay is that we know that we're all different. What does it matter, Melvin? We are all black, gay, and we live in the sticks."

"Yeah," Desmond added. "It's enough to have to battle with these Bible slinging saints around here who claim that all fags are going to hell. Why is it necessary that we have to battle on another?"

"It's not like you two are trying to get together or anything, are you?" Bradley asked.

"Hell no!" both Frederick and Melvin responded simultaneously.

"Then stop all of this craziness," Bradley said as he placed Mikki Howard's *Love Under New Management* cassette tape into the cassette player.

Music calms the savage beast.

Everyone in the car began to sing the lyrics to the song.

"All right," Desmond asked lightheartedly as the song came to an end. "Who is in love under new management tonight?"

"Xavier," everyone shouted in unison and began to laugh.

The atmosphere within the car began to change as they traveled closer to Memphis. When Mikki Howard finished several songs, the music was changed to the songs of Patti LaBelle, Prince, Anita Baker, Luther Vandros, and Freddie Jackson.

"O.K." Douglas said as he pulled the car onto Madison Avenue in Memphis, Tennessee. "You are about to get the scenic view of black gay life in metro Memphis."

The infamous *Apartment Club* was located on the corner of Madison Avenue and Union Avenue in Memphis, Tennessee. For Douglas, Danny Thomas Boulevard led the way to it but he passed the club and drove a block down to Union Avenue where the

Greyhound Bus Terminal was located; turned and traveled up Monroe Avenue where a multitude of gorgeous men walked slowly and gazed into the car. Douglas parked on Monroe and the group got out of the car. As the group slowly approached the club, Melvin noticed various people who walked down the sidewalk on the side of the club. There was a host of women who wore an assortment of finely outfits that began to enter the club. Some of these women wore two piece business suits that had splits up the back, up the sides, and some even, up the front of the skirts. Other of these women wore short formal gowns and were accompanies by a barrage of young men who carried suitcases, bags, and what looked like props in single filed lines behind these women. Melvin noticed every shade of black and every size of a woman yet he also noticed every style of a man begin to also approach the club. There were older men, younger men, middle aged men dressed in suits, sports attire, or simple slacks and shirts. There were men who entered who had definitely either worked out at the gym or had been recently released from prison who sported big chests and huge muscles who entered the club. There were also some men who loudly sashayed down the sidewalk only to join a group of onlookers who would laugh and cackle at the person who played the minstrel for the moment.

"I thought this was a gay club?" Melvin asked as he saw more women enter the club.

"This **is** a gay club!" Douglas, Bradley, and Frederick exclaimed in unison.

"Why are all of these women going into the club then?" Melvin asked earnestly.

Douglas, Bradley, and Frederick roared in laughter until tears began to stream from their eyes. It had been fortunate that Douglas had parked the car and they had exited or surely they would have had a wreck because Douglas literally held his sides in laughter.

"I don't get it," Melvin said.

"Me either," Desmond agreed. He personally could not understand why women would frequent a gay club either unless they were lesbians. Perhaps the club catered to lesbians more than gay men.

"They ain't women," Frederick blurted out. "They are drag queens, children."

"What?" Melvin gasped in stupefaction. He could not believe that the women who strolled down the sidewalk of Madison Avenue were actually men! Their nails, hair, make-up, and even figures suggested otherwise. They seemed so perfect.

"Miss Vincien," Frederick yelled as a tall, fair skinned, very attractive young man began to stroll past their group. The man quickly turned around towards Frederick. When he recognized Frederick, he approached him.

"Bitch," Vincien whispered as a horrified expression appeared on his face. "Don't **ever** call my name out in public!"

"Oh, I forgot," Frederick chuckled. "I just want to introduce you to my friends from home."

"I look hideous, guhl," Vincien commented as a shocked expression appeared on his face.

Bradley, Douglas, Desmond, and Melvin all stood and looked at the man that Frederick was attempting to introduce to the group.

"You look fabulous," Bradley laughed as he stretched forth his hand to shake Vincien's hand.

"Well, well, well, Miss Frederick," Vincien began as he looked Bradley over from head to toe as he shook the outstretched hand. "It seems to me that you have been holding back on me! What fine specimen of a man do we have here that brings such wonderful greetings to mother?" Vincien came close to gawking at Bradley. Bradley was indeed a very attractive man. On this evening, he wore a pair of tight fitting jeans that defined his round buttocks. The multicolored shirt that he chose was an opened v-neck that slightly revealed his smooth yet muscular chest.

"I'm Bradley, honey," Bradley chuckled as he hugged Vincien.

"Miss Frederick, child, I didn't realize that they make them this fine in that little country town that you are from... damn!" Vincien said as he hugged Bradley and looked him over once more.

"Well," Bradley chuckled and added in a high pitched womanly voice. "I do my best!" Vincien, although attractive, was not at all Bradley's type. Bradley felt that there was no need in misleading the man over a frivolous compliment. After living in Atlanta for a year, Bradley had begun to understand the mentality of the gay life style that had been established within the black gay culture. It was a culture that was very heterosexual in fact or was gauged by heterosexist standards. In this culture, there were men who claimed to be women because they were "bottoms" or the receptive partner during the course of anal sexual intercourse. There were men who were considered "butch." These men attempted to hide any feminine attribute. They were those who were "tops" and were the more passive person during the course of anal intercourse. Then, there were the "dykes" among the gay men. These were men who were "versatile" or enjoyed sex in either position. "Trade" was men who claimed to be straight or heterosexual but were actually bi-sexual men who enjoyed sex with homosexual men. There were the "drag queens" or men who dressed in women's clothes, some who performed during "The Show" or those who simply wore women's clothing. Then, there were the "drag kings" who were men who performed in "The Show" but did not wear women's clothing. A "Mother" within the culture usually referred to older gay men who took other gay men under his wing to teach him the ropes. "The Mother Board" was a group of older gay men in conference. A "Missionary" was a young gay man who had been out for a while, did noteworthy things, but had no "gay children." A Family consisted of a matriarch/patriarch who was bound together in some form. A House was a larger extension of a Family. The gay culture was very uniquely designed in the South and many understood practices occurred and were only understood by the black gay culture itself.

"O.K." Vincien said as he released Bradley and looked at the remaining members of the group. "Who do we have here, Frederick?"

"Guhl," Douglas laughed. "You know who I am!"

Vincien screamed, laughed, and then hugged Douglas.

"Where on earth have you been, Douglas?" Vincien asked. "I haven't seen you in ages, boy!"

"I'm in school in Jackson, Tennessee," Douglas said as he hugged Vincien again. "I got to Lane College!"

"You go, honey," Vincien said as he released his grip from Douglas. "More of these knuckle heads need to go to school and get the hell outta this club every damned weekend! Maybe they'll stop all of this damned stealing, robbing, and getting on that damned crack."

"Has it gotten that bad here?" Douglas asked sadly as he thought about his precious hometown.

"Child," Vincien explained. "Crack is beginning to run through the black gay community here so damned fast until it is unreal. Whoever invented that shit has to be a millionaire by now."

"Let me introduce you to Melvin and Desmond," Douglas said.

Melvin stepped forward to produce his hand to Vincien.

"How do you do?" Melvin greeted as Vincien grabbed his hand and then pulled him into a hug.

"I'm fine, guhl, how about you?" Vincien replied as he released Melvin.

"I'm fine," Melvin replied slightly apprehensively. He had never really hugged anyone that he was not intimate with before. Now, he was being hugged by a complete stranger. It didn't feel so bad but he still could not adjust to being called a girl. He had the feeling that his life would somehow change forever on this night.

Desmond immediately hugged Vincien and produced his name. Unlike Melvin, Desmond seemed to quickly embrace the gay culture without any difficulty.

"Well, children," Vincien interjected as he began to lead the group towards the doors of *The Apartment Club*. "I'm sure this is a first for some of you, but for whatever its worth, welcome to the exciting and colorful world of *The Apartment Club!* It's not the best club in the world... maybe the best club in the South, but it's owned, operated, and patronized by black gay people. Personally, I think it's the best club ever built here in Memphis. In here, you will meet people from every county in West Tennessee, most counties from northern

Mississippi, most counties from western Alabama, most counties from eastern Arkansas, people from Missouri come here, and people from Kentucky have made the trip to this club! If you just can't bear *The Apartment Club* on your first visit, you can always go over to *The Fourteen K* or if you prefer vanilla, you can always go to *J-Wags* or *George's*. For the faint at heart, this place definitely has to grow on you. You will definitely see many shocking things tonight!"

Melvin, listening intently to Vincien, knew that his life would change forever after this new experience. He knew that he was seconds away from crossing the threshold of a new world that he had never seen before.

Melvin became anxious.

His feelings were definitely warranted! When one crossed the threshold of *The Apartment Club* for the first time, a person usually had no choice but change forever. One either embraced the culture or totally rejected it and the greatest test always came within the walls of a large club that sat on the corner of Madison and Monroe Avenues in Memphis, Tennessee throughout the 1980s and for the beginning of the 1990s.

The small, dingy, dark and musty lobby was crowded with people. The inside of the club could not be seen from the outside like so many taverns that existed in the rural areas of West Tennessee.

Upon finally arriving to the entrance of the club through a small corridor, a fat, afro-wearing man blocked the entrance that led into the club.

"I.D." he said casually to Melvin who retrieved his driver's license from his back pocket and quickly passed it to the man. The man vaguely looked at Melvin's identification, much less the age that was printed plainly on it, before he returned it to Melvin.

"Three dollars," the man said flatly.

Melvin gave the man the money and crossed over into the world of *The Apartment Club*.

Melvin was not quite ready for the sight that he would behold.

There were beautiful, black men walking throughout the club. Tall men, short men, fat men, thin men, high yellow men, blue-black men, honey colored men, mustard colored men, chocolate colored men, caramel colored men... every hue, every build, every style, any flavor... all men who made up the universally labeled stamp of being... black!

Melvin's heart began to flutter!

Frederick, upon entrance, immediately walked to the bar. Melvin decided to tag along.

"Gimme some of that dishwater beer," Frederick teased the bartender.

"I can give you some dishwater beer, baby," the bartender teased. "But we do have draft for free until midnight tonight if that's what you'd like."

"And you know it," Frederick laughed. "Have you seen Billy?"

"Not tonight," the bartender replied.

"Tell him that I'm looking for him," Frederick chuckled as the bartender passed him a foaming cup full of beer. Frederick noticed Melvin behind him.

"The beer is free until twelve if you want some," Frederick said as he began to mingle in the crowd, leaving Melvin at the bar.

Melvin decided that he really needed a drink to calm his nerves at this point. Anything would be fine! He too ordered what Frederick had named "dishwater beer" since it was free. The beer, like the club, was not the best in the world. Actually, Melvin noted, it seemed rather flat, however, it refreshed his spirits and calmed his nerves.

Melvin began to walk toward the tables and chairs that sat directly in front of a massive stage. The group that he had come with had found a table and he decided to join them.

Melvin began to feel a great sense of pride. It was the first time in is life that he had been around so many men who were all black and were all gay. Perhaps they did not wave a gay flag but just taking the steps across the threshold of *The Apartment Club* symbolized it all.

"The show is gonna start in about thirty minutes, Melvin," Frederick said. "If you want anything else to drink you'd better go and get it now otherwise it is going to cost you."

"I'm straight," Melvin said as he sat beside Bradley and whispered... "What in the world is the show?"

"The show," Bradley explained. "Is when the drag queens lip sync to music of some great artist. They perform in pretty dresses and stuff. You just have to see it to understand it."

At midnight, The Show began.

Female impersonators or drag queens who were forthcoming legends entertained the crowd with an unmatched magnificence of the actual artist. Tamika St. James, Tamika St. John, Patti Cakes, Tanisha Cassidine, and Paula Poindexter were the reigning young entertainers of the season.

Melvin, like so many other gay men in the club, became mesmerized by the elegance, grace, and charm these men used during their performance. All of the performers wore elegant evening gowns – not just any evening gown – but expensive gowns. It was nothing to see these men perform in sequin, lace, velvet, and even fur. The gowns would be elaborately bejeweled with one specific item that stood out above all of the rest. The performers usually wore pounds of make-up. Yes, pounds rather than mounds. These performers went to great length to make themselves look exactly like women. In so doing, their faces had to be perfect because the competition among the drag queens from *The Apartment Club* was so fierce that nothing short of excellence was allowed on stage. Further, it was unheard of and a cardinal sin for a drag queen to perform without a "beat" hairdo. Hence, Melvin saw everything from high bouffants to bobs that were cropped so close to the head that you could see the straightened strands. Indeed, they were glamorous. So glamorous, in fact, that Melvin began to change his opinion and position about the "gay scene."

Paula Poindexter began to perform Anita Baker's *no More Tears*. Paula in her red beaded dress that revealed her legs that would openly put Tina Turner's legs to shame choreographed the number so well until Melvin became totally enthralled with her. He could almost feel the pain of the voice from the music. The story that was told in song yet performed by Paula began to deeply touch the pit of Melvin's inner being. He could not contain himself. He just had to touch her. He noticed that other people were giving the performer dollar bills. He stood up, reached into his wallet, withdrew a dollar, and walked toward the stage.

"Where in the hell are you going? Frederick asked.

"I can't help it," Melvin said. "I've got to tip this heffa something. This wench knows she is working the hell out of this song in that damned beaded dress!"

As Melvin walked toward the stage, gave the performer a dollar, he hugged Paula Poindexter. Paula returned the hugged but kept performing and collecting dollar bills.

Everyone at Melvin's table stared at him in disbelief and shock.

"I told him" Frederick laughed. "*The Apartment Club* will draw you or drive you!"

The group laughed.

"What's so funny?" Melvin asked as he returned to the table.

"Oh," Frederick laughed. "I just made a comment about how certain experiences have a way of changing us. Welcome to the gay world, Melvin."

"What did I do wrong?" Melvin asked self consciously.

"Child," Bradley said. "You didn't do anything wrong. We are just tripping on the fact that you were ready to persecute gay people earlier tonight and you just tipped the gayest acting of us all!"

"I couldn't help myself," Melvin admitted. "That saint was sanging!"

"Correction," Frederick teased. "She was performing!"

The announcer announced a new entertained to the stage that had come to Memphis from Atlanta. The entertainer chose to performer Stephanie Mill's *Home*. Ordinarily, Memphis and *The Apartment Club* patrons would welcome any newcomer to the stage, however, the crowd had expected a fierce performance from the entertainer because the guy was from Atlanta - at least he claimed that he was. Second, *Home* had been performed on stage of *The Apartment Club* by drag queens that literally looked exactly as Stephanie did when she made a video. The legends of *The Apartment Club* would perform the song in a white laced dressed with hair that was straightened and curled on the tip ends.

The new performer from Atlanta chose a green formal that looked too big. She was slow and stiff and seemingly did not know the words to the music.

The crowd became disinterested immediately.

Bradley was horrified. This creature claimed that he was from Atlanta and Bradley knew damned well that the performers were better than this.

A drag queen who sat in the audience watched the performance from the edge of the stage. Finally, the second drag queen could no longer stand the bad performance.

"Bitch," the drag queen who stood on the side of the stage said. "You ain't doing this shit right. Let me show you how to do Miss Stephanie Mills, honey!"

"Sit down, Miss Covington," someone from the audience yelled.

"Boo!" someone else yelled as "Miss Covington" began to twirl around the stage yelling "Dis is how you do it, bitch" which totally ruined the shocked performer's act.

Vincien laughed so hard until he fell out of his chair.

"What in the world is going on?" Desmond asked.

"That crazy Miss Tyrone Covington keeps these girls in line," Frederick laughed. "He can't take a bad performance and this one is fucking *Home* up badly!"

"That bitch was crazy for even trying to perform *Home*, honey," Vincien said. "Everybody knows that's my damned song. I'm happy Miss Covington got that ass!"

Melvin was shocked again. Vincien had revealed a new revelation. Melvin could not believe that he was sitting at the table with… a drag queen in men's clothing.

The show ended and the house music began to thump throughout the club.

Desmond and Douglas headed to the dance floor holding hands.

"Did I miss something?" Melvin asked as he noticed the two of them.

"It looks like they are becoming an item," Bradley chuckled.

"All right, bitch," Frederick said as he jumped out of his chair. "I'll see y'all in a minute. I see some dick that I've gotta go chase!"

"Let the dick chase you, honey," Vincien laughed as he stood up, looked around the club, walked to a group that was obviously his friends, and began to talk.

"Let's go dance, Melvin," Bradley said. "This music has got it going on!"

"Sure," Melvin said as he followed Bradley to the lower dance floor.

Once again, this was a new experience for Melvin. He had never danced with a man before in his life. He quickly realized, though, that it was exactly like dancing with a woman. The dance floor was totally packed with people. Melvin glanced over his shoulders and noticed that there were people actually *Voguing* in front of the mirror.

"Watch out for the twirlers," Bradley warned Melvin as a guy danced passed them and then kicked his leg high into the air and then began to dance harder.

Melvin was slightly envious of some of the dancers. They could kick and twirl and move into some exotic/erotic motion and then suddenly *Vogue* and then end with a split only to begin a totally new dance. He didn't know why he was shocked at Bradley's performance either. Bradley was just as erotic and provocative as the other dancers were. He never missed a beat to the ever changing music. It seemed that the louder and deeper the drum beats thundered, the more provocative Bradley became.

"I'm tired," Melvin lied after about the twelfth song had played.

"Cool, go ahead," Bradley said as he turned away from Melvin, twirled around, did a run way walk, and then kicked. After he kicked, he landed back on his feet whereas he began to *Vogue..*

With all of the fine, young, black, gorgeous men in the club, Melvin strangely began to feel alone as he walked toward an open room that appeared to be a lounge area. Several people darted in and out of the room. A wide screened television set sat in the middle of it. Melvin looked onto the television screen to see what was actually playing. To his amazement, he saw two sexy black men having sex.

"This is no room for me," he thought and decided to leave the room before he could even think about getting an erection.

Just as he was about to leave the room, the dj slowed the music down and Prince began to croon the first bars of *Adore.*

"Damn, that's my favorite song and I have no one to dance with," Melvin commented to himself yet the words seemed to automatically flow from his lips. He could not help but feel a slight tinge of jealousy as he noticed the dance floor become packed with couples who had begun to slow dance.

"It's my favorite song too," a deep and sexy voice said which startled Melvin.

Melvin froze.

He knew that he had heard the voice and it seemed as if it were coming from behind him. *"Surely this person cannot be talking to me,"* Melvin thought as he turned around and looked directly into the eyes of a very fine, chocolate specimen that human's entitled… a man.

The Heaven's stood still for Melvin, so it seemed. This man *was* actually talking to him. And yet, Prince continued his litany.

"Would you like to dance?" the guy asked.

"Indeed," Melvin replied as he grabbed the extended hand of this stranger and was led to the dance floor.

The man felt so good to Melvin.

The man looked so fine to Melvin.

The man's Lagerfeld smelled so good to Melvin. Melvin was no stranger to Lagerfeld as his father had begun to wear it.

The man was tall.

"Hallelujah!" Melvin thought as he slid his arms around the man's neck, laid his head on the man's muscular chest, and closed his eyes as Prince continued to sing.

The guy placed on e hand around Melvin's waist and the other on Melvin's buttock.

Melvin's heart and nature began to stir as he felt as if he were in Seventh Heaven at this moment.

Finally Prince crooned the last bars of *Adore* but the dj continued his tribute to lovers with Luther Vandross's *if Only for One Night.*

Melvin could not help but scream. He loved Luther's music. He loved being held by this man. He wanted to dance the night away in this man's arms.

"What's your name?" the guy asked.

"Melvin," Melvin replied. "What's yours?"

"Julian," he replied

"What a beautiful name," Melvin said as he closed his eyes, rested his head on Julian's shoulder, and danced to the melodious beat and music being played.

"Not as beautiful are you are right now," Julian whispered to Melvin and drew him closer.

Melvin felt weak!

His legs seemed like jell-o and he knew that if he released his hold on Julian he surely would fall into the middle of the dance floor.

They continued to dance through Luther's *If Only for One Night* and throughout *And It's Gonna Be Tonight.*

Melvin giggled slightly.

"Are you sure it's gonna be tonight?" Julian whispered into Melvin's ear.

"What are you talking about?" Melvin asked as once again, his heart skipped a beat. *"Did I hear him right? Is he propositioning me?"* Melvin thought.

"Can we be together tonight?" Julian asked.

Melvin lifted his head off of Julian's shoulder where he could get a good look at this man in whom he embraced so closely and yet did not know him.

"I don't think so," Melvin said.

Julian was about four inches taller than Melvin. He wore a low cut fade and had a very meticulously shaped goatee. The almost pencil thin eyebrows sat atop two of the most gorgeous dark brown eyes that Melvin had ever seen before in his life. His nose was not big nor was it small. It almost seemed perfect. His lips were full and voluptuous.

Melvin inwardly had a battle within himself. His nature said: *"Hell yeah, go and get fucked by this man!"* His rural upbringing said: *"You just met this man and you don't know shit about him. He could be an ax murderer for all you know!"*

With that thought, Melvin said: "I really don't know you well enough to go to bed with you."

Julian grinned and squeezed Melvin tightly which made Melvin almost regret that he had said anything.

"I don't want you to go to bed with me right now," Julian said. "I want you to go out to eat with me after we leave the club."

"Oh," Melvin said noticing that he had said that he didn't want to go to bed with him *right now*. This only meant that he did want to go to bed with him. Melvin actually wanted to jump up and say *Hallelujah* but instead said. "I came with friend."

The slow music ended.

The house music began to thunder through the club again.

The embrace ended.

Melvin suddenly felt naked and insecure.

"Can I get your number?" Julian asked.

"Sure, but I believe I already have yours," Melvin said in an attempt to sound sexy yet mature.

Julian laughed.

Julian grabbed Melvin's hand and led him into the room where the television played porno. The two of them talked for the rest of the night.

Melvin could not believe that he had finally met someone who genuinely had an interest in him. He also could not believe that he had met someone that had begun to dissipate the long and tedious crush that he had for The Rev. For Melvin, Julian would provide him with a closer connection to himself because Julian recognized the fact that he was gay and wanted to be with another gay man.

During the course of the conversation, Melvin discovered that he had far more in common than he thought with Julian. Then, Melvin learned that Julian was from Jackson, Tennessee!

"Hot damn!" Melvin thought. *"I praise God through it all!"*

And then… it happened.

Julian looked into Melvin's eyes and kissed him.

Melvin, needing to end his streak of loneliness, returned the kiss.

Usually, Melvin did not kiss in public. He thought it was rather taboo but for the first time in his life, he did not care!

He wanted to taste every part of Julian from the crown of his head to the soul of his feet and every part in between. For once, he could care less what society had to say. Then he realized that within this particular society, no one cared.

Julian began to kiss Melvin so passionately until Melvin felt as if the stars would fall from the sky all around him.

"Melvin," a voice rang out as Melvin's arms wrapped tightly around Julian's neck and Julian's tongue darted deeply into his throat. "We've been looking all over for you!"

Melvin vaguely heard the voice as he was totally enthralled and mesmerized by this Julian person. The voice seemed like a distant whisper on a distant shore while he stood on one shore and an ocean stood between him and the voice.

"Did you hear me?" Bradley yelled as he tapped Melvin on the shoulder.

"What?" Melvin said as he slowly tore away from Julian's embrace in order to adjust his mind and then face Bradley.

"We are getting ready to go because the club has closed," Bradley said.

"Shit," Julian said.

"Damn," Melvin said.

Julian escorted Melvin to Douglas's car.

Melvin introduced Julian to the group.

"I live in Jackson," Julian reminded Melvin. "I can take you back to Lane."

"Well, Melvin said. "I'm not going back to Jackson tonight. I actually live in Fairhaven."

"Well," Julian chuckled. "I can take you back to Fairhaven, then. I am really feeling you and don't want you to get away from me for a long period of time."

Melvin thought about it. In his mind, it seemed s if it took him an hour to process the entire matter. In reality, it took him no greater than five seconds. He did not know what to do. One voice told him: *Go home with the people that you came with.* His heart said: *Take a chance on Julian and go home with Julian.* His manhood said: *Take a chance on Julian and go home with him.* The vote was two-to-one.

"Hey, guy," Melvin said as he stepped out of the car and then looked at Desmond, Douglas, Frederick, and Bradley. "Julian is going to give me a ride home. I'll talk with you all tomorrow."

Melvin could tell by the expressions on his friends' faces that they were indeed shocked.

"Close your mouths," Melvin said as he looked at them. "This ain't the first time you've seen a man leave with another man!"

"You go, bitch," Frederick laughed as he walked passed Douglas' car to a car that was parked directly behind it. "I got a date too, so I'm leaving with somebody else too! I'll holla when I holla!"

Bradley shook his head.

Douglas cranked up the car and sped off.

Julian convinced Melvin to ride home with him to Jackson, Tennessee. He promised to take Melvin back to Fairhaven the next day.

One their way to Jackson, they discussed their backgrounds further; their future aspirations; and their feelings about the gay life and culture. Melvin's heart began to warm to this man named Julian. He prayed that Julian would have a more permanent place in his life. Although he was horny as hell, he really wanted more than a one night stand.

Julian was kind, compassionate, and easy to talk to. He listened intently to Melvin and Melvin listened intently to him. Melvin learned that he was twenty-two years old. He was a junior at Union University in Jackson. He worked in the office at Proctor and Gamble factory as a data processor. He had his own apartment. He owned the black 1989 Chrysler LeBaron that they rode in heading to Jackson. He was a member in good standing at Macedonia Baptist Church in Jackson and he was President of the youth N.A.A.C.P.

"What are you looking for?" Melvin finally asked sincerely.

"I think I've already found him," Julian replied. "And in the least of all places... *The Apartment Club.*"

Melvin, though warmed by his words, needed more than a remark that made him feel good.

Melvin laughed lightly.

"Seriously," Melvin asked. "What are you really looking for?"

"Again," Julian replied. "I think I've already found him."

Julian pulled his car into the *Old Hickory Apartments*. He turned the ignition of the car of but allowed the music to play. Anita Baker sang *Giving You the Best That I've Got.*

Julian looked into Melvin's eyes.

"I'm looking for a man just like you, Melvin," he said as he grabbed Melvin's hand and began to tenderly caress it. "I want somebody who wants something out of life. I'm looking for a man who I can love and who can love me in return. In a minute, I'm going to turn the key to my apartment, I want a man, who even if he doesn't live with me, I will know in my heart that I am no longer alone. Do you think you can fit that bill?"

"Can birds fly?' Melvin answered.

"Touché," Julian said as he kissed Melvin.

Chapter Eight
I Get Joy When I Think About It

What troubles have we seen?
What conflicts have we passed?
Fightings without, and fears within,
Since we assembled last!
But out of all the Lord
Has brought us by His love;
And still He does His help afford,
And hides our life above.

"What in the hell were you doing last night?" Bradley yelled into the telephone receiver when finally Melvin answered on the fifth ring "And what time did you get in?"

"I don't understand the question?" Melvin yawned as he turned over to look at the clock that read nine-thirty-five.

"You left the club last night with a man that you didn't have an inkling or a clue of who he was," Bradley began. "What time did you get home and have you lost your mind?"

"Get used to knowing his name, Bradley," Melvin said. "His name is Julian Jordan and he is my new lover and what time I got in is my business."

"You just met the man last night," Bradley continued.

"The things that man did to my body last night," Melvin gigged as he turned over in the bed and pulled the sheet up over his head.

"And you all call me a Tramp," Bradley laughed. "Well, I hope that it was good for you. I'm happy that you are happy!"

"Oh, it was good," Melvin giggled like a child who had just received his first awaited bicycle. "Bradley, he made me feel so special. He was slow and gentle and oh my goodness. I have never felt like this before in my life. He was so caring and loving and gentle."

"Child, don't get too excited over this new relationship," Bradley advised. "You have to bear in mind, he is your first! You will soon discover that men will definitely break your heart... especially those that you meet at the club."

"Not this one," Melvin argued. "He is so wonderful and we have so many things in common. We think so much alike until it is funny."

"Child, I know I need to get back to Hotlanta," Bradley laughed. "You have gotten your first piece of thang and now you are sprung like a mug! I do hope that he doesn't hurt you. Promise me that you will just be careful and take things slow!"

"I promise," Melvin said. He didn't think that he had to make this promise to Bradley because Julian was everything and more than he had hoped for in a man.

"Whatever happened to your infatuation with The Rev, anyway?" Bradley inquired.

"Forget The Rev," Melvin said quickly. "The only thing that kept me infatuated with him was the fact that we kissed and he let me suck his horse dick!"

"What?" Bradley asked. "When in the hell did this happen and why wasn't I informed?"

"It happened during our junior year in high school at the New Year's Eve Ball," Melvin explained.

"At the Ball? The O.P.T. Ball?" Bradley yelled in excitement. "Tragedy! For the shame of it all!"

"Wasn't no shame or tragedy in it, honey," Melvin mused. "The Rev had the dick of death on him, child, and I had to have it."

"*Jezebel!*" Bradley roared in laughter. "I'm just too through! How in the hell did you keep that major secret from me for so long? No wonder you always wanted to defend and protect his precious honor!"

"I was in love with him," Melvin confessed. "He didn't love me. No, he could not love me the way that I needed to be loved. I deserve much more than that, Bradley. So, to hell with him. It's not too much for me to want to be loved is it, Bradley?"

"Of course not, baby," Bradley said. "And you definitely deserve to be loved. That's the reason that I steer clear of love and matters of the heart. Some people can get you all worked up and involved in their world and the next thing you know, they leave you!"

"Is that what happened to you?" Melvin asked. "Or is that why you never take relationships seriously?"

"I just don't want to be tied down to any one individual," Bradley explained. "People will expect all of these great expectations out of you because they are chasing some fantasy. Then, in order to get you to be what they want you to be, they will start trying to mold you into somebody that they want you to be. Then, after you mold into what they want you to be, you realize that you have lost yourself and to discover that they really didn't want the fantasy anyway. Me, personally, I don't allow my trade to cross certain boundaries. This is why it is so much easier for me to just tell a person what I am or am not trying to get into: *If you want me it will certainly cost you.* I have absolutely no problems when they realize that I am an expensive 'ho, therefore, I cannot be tamed or conditioned into that terrible thing that you are so madly chasing called a damned relationship!"

"I admire your strength," Melvin said.

"What strength?" Bradley asked. "I have no strength but I do have determination. Because I know best at how to please me, I am comfortable being alone. Eventually, I may settle down to one individual but it will be on my terms and my terms alone. Just look at how crazy Frederick was when Howard left him. Howard has gone on with is life and Frederick still hasn't gotten over him."

"That was so foul how it happened too," Melvin commented as he thought about the break-up between Frederick and Howard. The story goes that Frederick met a mutual friend who was almost an exact replica of himself. One night, the friend called him over to his apartment. He told Frederick that the door would be unlocked. When

Frederick went over to the apartment he went inside only to discover Howard and the man in bed together.

"Not really," Bradley stated. "Frederick knew that Howard was bored with their relationship. You can't tell me that Frederick never saw the signs. Howard obviously did not want to be tied down any further. He seemed to feel that if he smothered Howard with a lot of sex then Howard would remain. Take my advice, if you want to run a man away, smother him and he will leave you no matter how good you think your stuff is."

"I'm not stuttin' you, "Melvin laughed. "When are you leaving for Atlanta?"

"I'm leaving tonight at midnight," Bradley replied.

"You take care of yourself," Melvin said.

"And you know that," Bradley chuckled. "Give me a call whenever you need anything, Melvin! And don't be a damned stranger!"

Melvin was silent.

"Did you hear me, Melvin?" Bradley asked.

"Yes, I hear you," Melvin said. "I won't be a stranger and I will call you if I need anything. It just seems like the tide is finally turning. That's kind of funny to me."

"I need to have it printed in *The State Gazette, The Jackson Sun,* and *The Commercial Appeal* that you finally got a man," Bradley chuckled. "Lord knows you are well over due. I just hope that this Julian Jordan character is right for you!"

"Right now," Melvin grinned. "I don't even care!"

Against Bradley's advice, Melvin fell head over heels in love with Julian Jordan in a mere six weeks. For Melvin, Julian was everything that he had ever desired in a man. He was tall handsome, articulate, and professionally yet meticulously dressed at all times. His demeanor demanded him to be able to handle any situation at any given time. He could easily adjust to new surroundings. He handled problematic situations with ease. His presence was strong and powerful. He was an active leader in his school church and community. Whatever he put his mind and thoughts to conquer, he did! Prior to sex with Julian, Melvin had actually been a virgin. Julian's animalistic behavior in bed prodded Melvin into becoming more open and attentive. Because Melvin had never truly experienced sex, Julian constantly took him to new levels. Conversations with Julian ranged from the most trivial to the most advanced and he never tired of hearing himself speak. Julian showered Melvin with attention personally yet it was understood that he never showed emotion in public. Melvin felt that he had *it all* in this man named Julian Jordan.

Because of Julian's aggressive concerns with the community, he had begun to enter the political arena and be taught by some of the most prolific politicians in Tennessee. He was no stranger to lunch with the Governor of Tennessee, State Representatives, State Senators, U.S. Congressmen, the mayor of Jackson, presidents of the local universities, staunch Republicans, staunch Democrats – anyone who had political power knew the name and face of Julian Jordan. Melvin, like everyone else in Jackson, knew that one day Julian would become a powerful governmental official of some kind. At Union, his undergraduate degree was Political Science. He had already applied to several law schools in Tennessee and was presently waiting acceptance. Julian could always be seen on the campuses of Union University, Lane College, Lambuth University or even Jackson State Community College in the midst of any conflict, fighting for some great cause, or fighting for the rights of some individual that he felt had been unjustly treated.

Everyone within the metro Jackson, Tennessee area knew the name and face of Julian Jordan. His charm and eloquent demeanor commanded the respect of anyone in whom he came in contact with. He reminded Melvin of The Rev in so many ways. Being with Julian was almost like watching The Rev in action in Omega Phi Theta but only on a larger scale. Julian, unlike The Rev, was not limited to a fraternity although both were well known throughout West Tennessee. Melvin loved the fact that he, yes, he, was dating such a man! His Julian was not an obvious homosexual to the scrutinizing eye of the public. Although Julian had committed to him during the throws of passion, their relationship was not one that was obvious to the public. In fact, their relationship was very similar to the relationship of Xavier and the Reverend William Barnes yet Melvin felt that somehow it was better. Unlike Xavier, though, Melvin did not travel with Julian like Xavier traveled with William.

"How is the Reverend Doctor?" Melvin asked Xavier one day as they sat in Melvin's dorm room.

"Wonderful," Xavier said as a huge grin appeared upon his face. Like Melvin, Xavier was rather smitten too. "How is the future Mister President?"

"Absolutely marvelous," Melvin giggled. "These are the best days of my life!"

"He's dickin' you down that good, huh?" Desmond interrupted as he entered the dorm room.

"You are one to talk," Melvin laughed. "How are things going with you and Douglas?"

"He's slowly growing on me," Desmond said as he dropped down on his bed with a large bag containing donuts, cookies, candy bars, potato chips, and three sodas.

Xavier and Melvin looked at one another in disbelief and then they looked at Desmond who seemed oblivious to them. Unfortunately, Desmond could not easily be read when it came to matters of the heart. This was definitely a time when they could not fully understand exactly where his mind was. For them, love was essential and both of them were enjoying the springtime of new love and romance.

"Is something wrong with you and Douglas?" Melvin found the words to finally ask

"Of course not," Desmond said as he opened a package of donuts and then a can of soda and began to munch on the donuts allowing white powder to encase his mouth. "Why on earth would you ask me a question like that?"

"You all are still *growing* on one another?" Xavier questioned in astonishment.

"Yeah," Desmond said as he looked expressionlessly into the face of both Melvin and Xavier. "Douglas has his way of doing things and my way is totally different. We are adjusting to this but I am really beginning to care for him. I just want to get to know him and I am happy that he just wants to get to know me on several different levels. Hell, we just had sex a couple of nights ago."

Both Melvin and Xavier's eyes bulged in shock.

"Yeah," Desmond giggled. "The one thing that I explained to Douglas was the fact that I was still a virgin and if I gave myself to him, I was doing it for the long haul and not just a random fuck that he could get from anybody. I gave him the freedom of getting whatever he needed but I told him, once he entered me, I'd kill his ass if ever he got with anybody else. Because I was adamant, I decided that we should wait until I felt something. He agreed but didn't cheat on me."

"How did you know that he didn't?" Xavier asked.

"He didn't have time to," Desmond chuckled and then opened a candy bar and began to eat it. "He was with me everywhere I have been except for in class. When he wasn't with me, he was at work. We decided to shoot for building a future together rather than just fucking."

A slight pang of jealousy stabbed at Melvin's heart. He had been with Julian for six glorious weeks. They had had sex continuously for at least four of those weeks. Never had the thought occurred to Melvin that they should build a future together nor had Julian ever mentioned the possibilities. Melvin had attended so many religious, community, or political functions with Julian until he had totally lost count. No one ever questioned why Melvin "tagged" along during all of these events. It was assumed that because Melvin's father was the owner of a funeral home, that Melvin, like Julian, had aspirations of a political seat as well. Recently, Julian had announced that he was running for some public office that had a seat in Nashville or Knoxville, hence; for the past two weeks, Melvin and Julian had not really enjoyed one private alone. The only place Julian had not been followed was when he announced to the pursuing crowd that he was tired and was going home to retire for the evening. Usually, but not always, this was Melvin's clue to meet him at his apartment for a round of hot, raunchy, sweaty, yet passionate sex – the kind that was definitely considered an abomination by the church!

Xavier sat and thought about his relationship with Rev. William Barnes. Because Xavier sang so well, he was always a welcome surprise before William preached. Hence, Xavier had been to endless church services with William that always ended with wild, untamed, hot, sweaty yet passionate sex in some motel room after the services. Xavier, one who had stopped going to church, found himself attending everything from Sunday morning worship services, to programs at varying times on Sunday afternoon, to Sunday evening services, to mid week services, to full week revival services, and most recently to an ice-cream social and calendar tea with William. Dinner was always eaten at any family restaurant between Tennessee, Arkansas, and Mississippi that served buffets. It never matter what name was given to the place, if the food was hot or cold, good or bad, as long as the meal was never in excess of $6.99 per plate, William gladly chose this for himself and a begrudging Xavier. On the other hand, traveling with William during those previous six weeks to various conventions, revivals, musicals, and various programs had become advantageous to a new project that Xavier had begun. He had begun to train his voice to sing professionally with the help of the choral director from Lane College. Slowly, Xavier's fame had begun to spread as the prelude singer to this great preacher from either Arkansas or Tennessee. Yet, after listening to Desmond's words, the feelings that Xavier had developed for William were almost eradicated yet Xavier knew that William's popularity had begun to grow by leaps and bounds throughout the National Baptist Convention.

"Well," Desmond said as he began to rattle wrappers from the food that he had eaten. He placed them into a nearby waste basket and then retrieved clean underwear and a towel. "I've got to get rolling and head to the showers and take a shower. Douglas and I are heading to Paris Landing tonight to celebrate our one month anniversary."

Melvin looked at Xavier.

Xavier looked at Melvin.

It seemed as if cold water had been dashed into both of their faces.

Suddenly, the in unison, screamed with such velocity until it frightened Desmond enough to turn around in an attempt to figure out what was wrong with the two. He didn't know if they had seen a mouse or a snake or if perhaps the building had caught fire suddenly.

"One month anniversary at Paris Landing?" Melvin begrudgingly managed to question. "When exactly did you two officially become a couple?"

"Oh, Desmond responded and once again began to head for the showers. "About two weeks after both of you fell head over heels in love with the characters you are with."

"I knew it," Xavier exclaimed.

"Oh, do you?" Desmond said as he turned around, closed the dorm room door, and then sat down on his bed. "Do you really want to know the whole story?"

"Do we want to know all of what, Desmond?" Melvin asked as he raised one eyebrow and perked both ears in anticipation of hearing some juicy gossip.

Desmond looked at Xavier and Melvin. He shook his head.

"Please," Xavier said as he noticed the slight sadness within Desmond's eyes. "Inform us!"

"Are you sure that you wanna hear this?" Desmond asked. "Are you sure that you can handle it?"

"Desmond," Melvin fussed. "If you don't tell us what in the world you are talking about I will be forced to fight you and you know that I don't fight anyone."

Desmond smiled and waved his hand in protest at Melvin.

"I can't stand it either," Xavier yelled. "Please tell us what's up. Desmond?"

"O.K." Desmond said. "You two broke our hearts!"

"What?" Melvin ad Xavier screamed in unison.

"Melvin," Desmond continued expressionlessly. "Douglas wanted you so badly until he could literally taste you. I actually believe that he thought that you were the best thing since homemade ice-cream. He never really knew how to tell you!"

Melvin began to feel weak at his knees. He thanked God that he was sitting on his own bed.

"He tried everything in the world in an attempt to get you to see it," Desmond continued. "Do you remember all of the times that he took you to the movies, or roller skating at the skating rink, or bowling, or out to eat, or ever to his house in Memphis to meet his family?"

"Yes, but..." Melvin whispered in confusion.

"That was his way," Desmond explained.

"Well why in the hell didn't he just say something?" Xavier blurted out in an attempt to defend Melvin's injured pride.

"He was going to the night that we all went out to *The Apartment Club*," Desmond said. "But, Julian beat him to the punch!"

"But," Melvin defended. "I thought that you two were together on that night. I saw him when he held your hand and led you to the dance floor!"

"He was introducing me to somebody," Desmond said. "Plus, it was a fast song and when we found you again you were all hugged up with Julian on the dance floor. I could not let Douglas be hurt like that."

"I didn't mean to hurt him or anybody else that night," Melvin confessed earnestly.

"Melvin," Desmond said. "You left the club that night with a man that you had just met. Child, how could he not be anything else but hurt?"

"I did leave with Julian," Melvin acknowledged.

"Well," Xavier said boldly in an attempt to pry further. "Since you were the only other person left, how did I hurt you?"

"Xavier," Desmond said as he looked Xavier directly in the eyes. "I wanted to be with you every since we all got to Lane!"

"What?" Xavier and Melvin screamed in unison again.

Desmond stood up, gathered his clothes, and walked out of the dorm room. Strangely, however, his attitude and expression changed as he closed the door. He seemed to have relieved himself of a heavy burden upon revealing this hidden secret.

Xavier and Melvin were stunned into silence.

"One month anniversary at Paris Landing," Melvin said wryly as he looked at the telephone receiver and thought about the fact that Julian had recently called and canceled a private dinner they had scheduled weeks ago.

"Tonight is my six weeks anniversary, child," Xavier grimly commented softly.

"Our men," Melvin chuckled sarcastically.

"I don't know how much longer I can play this *preacher's wife* role, Melvin," Xavier confessed. "It's really beginning to drive me fucking insane!"

"Well, Xavier," Melvin asked. "Do you really think that being a politician's beau is much better?"

"I didn't come all the way to Tennessee," Xavier began to cry. "To become some preacher's whore. I can sing damn it and I promise you, Melvin James, that I am going to become somebody in this world before I die."

"You are already somebody," Melvin comforted. "You cannot let anybody take you away from you, though, Xavier!"

"I thought you had a date, Melvin?" Xavier asked and then looked into Melvin's eyes. "Oh, he cancelled again. Humph!"

"Yes," Melvin said. "He cancelled."

"I wonder what if…" Xavier thought aloud but fought hard to abandon the thoughts of his inner most feelings.

"Things will get better," Melvin said in an attempt to console his friend's wounded spirit and his damaged pride.

Things did get better!

Douglas and Desmond soon became the envy of Melvin's inner circle of friends that he was associated with during his Lane College experience. They had taken their relationship slowly whereas they truly began to appreciate the values possessed be the other person. Douglas took the time out to learn the simple things about Desmond that made Desmond happy, sad, argumentative, consoling, passionate, or those things that turned Desmond totally off. In retrospect, Desmond discovered all of the intimate things about Douglas that he had shared with no one. An unbreakable bond grew between them whereas it soon became common to ask one of them a question and before the person in whom you asked the question could get his statement out, the alternative person had completed it. By the end of their sophomore year at Lane College, the two had moved into an apartment together and, consequently, entered the work force. Because of this entry into the work force, obtaining a degree from Lane suddenly became secondary to them both. Desmond withdrew from Lane at the end of the semester and then applied and was accepted into *McCollum & Ross Cosmetology School*. *McCollum and Ross Cosmetology School*, like Lane, was also located in Jackson, Tennessee. Hence, during the day Desmond went to school in order to complete a cosmetology degree while he worked at *Sears* at *The Old Hickory Mall of Jackson* during the evenings. Douglas, on the other hand, had his fill completely of the collegiate world and Lane. He was promoted to the position of store manager of the pizza parlor that he had worked at in Jackson since his arrival there. Because the responsibility had become greater as a manager, there was little or no time to juggle a relationship and a course load at Lane. The money he had begun to make within the pizza industry was more than he had ever made in his life.

Both Melvin and Xavier lamented the fact that Desmond and Douglas had withdrawn from Lane College. They were slightly disturbed that Desmond and Douglas chose the work force over a degree. They were both shocked that Desmond and Douglas had leased an apartment together and had already begun to fill it with leased furniture. The latter made it a must for them to work when at

Lane, that was unnecessary. Melvin and Xavier did not, however, lament the opportunity to become dormitory mates at Lane.

"Why would you quit school?" Melvin begged Desmond for an explanation.

"You know that I'm multi-talented, Melvin," Douglas chuckled. "I have always done hair on the side and I have always played the piano for somebody's church. It will only take me a year to complete this course and then get my license. You know that my Aunt Flora died and left me her shop and I really need to do something with it. Plus, I never stopped playing for St. James either and they finally raised my salary to $75 a week."

"I know that you are not serious about going back to Fairhaven or Newbern?" Melvin asked in disgust as well as surprise.

"That is an option," Desmond commented as he packed the last of his belongings.

"You have become so much more, Desmond, damn it," Melvin argued. "Why do you have to drop out of school?"

"In case you haven't realized it," Desmond offered casually. "McCollum and Ross is a school. Plus, you keep forgetting that, like so many other black colleges, Lane is a private institution and these fees are putting me further and further in debt."

"You have passing grades," Melvin persisted. "There are always scholarships available."

Desmond squarely looked Melvin in the face in order to emphasis his point.

"I am NOT coming back to Lane," Desmond said. "Is that understood?"

"I just feel that you are throwing your life away for a man," Melvin said.

The room went deadly silent.

Melvin remembered the old saying: *There is calm before the storm!* He had never truly crossed Desmond yet there was always a first time for everything. He was insistent, however, that he cared about his friend's future. Both knew that an inevitable war was brewing in the Middle East. Melvin felt that presently, the only protection many black men in their age range had was to remain in higher education whereas if a draft occurred, they would not be included. From time to time, he had begun to hear about friends from high school who had enlisted in the military that were on their way to Kuwait. As a young black man, especially a young gay man, the season was sketchy and uncertainty had begun to cloud the minds of many young people. Most of their fathers had served the military in Vietnam. The ever brewing crisis in the Middle East was always a present thought in the minds of young black men. Melvin knew that, although he had lived a life of somewhat privilege, many of his friends did not have that luxury, hence, if a draft occurred, like Vietnam, most of his friends would be drafted to fight in a new war on strange shores.

"I am throwing my life away for a man?" Desmond laughed in disbelief. "I can't believe that you just said that shit. How dare you!"

Melvin could not believe that he had said it either yet he had.

"You can live off campus and still attend school," Melvin attempted in order to neutralize a forthcoming possible situation.

"First of all," Desmond said as the countenance of a demon seemed to appear on his face. "I am sick to death of being around these pretentious hypocrites here at Lane! Second, you know damned well that Douglas is a good man! He is far better than that piece of a man that you have. Oh, and by the way, when was the last time Mr. Julian Jordan even acknowledged your presence in public or even in private as far as that's concerned?"

Melvin was speechless! Desmond, the quiet one in Melvin's circle of friends, had just *read* him. Melvin knew that Douglas was indeed a good man and therefore would be a great provider for Desmond and anything close to a family that they may achieve. Melvin had watched Douglas bend over backward for Desmond throughout the course of the years in order to prove his love and affection. There was never a time when Melvin could not remember Desmond receiving flowers, expensive cologne, or an invitation to go to some private and remote place with Douglas. Truly, Douglas treated Desmond like a king/queen and in retrospect, there was never a time that Melvin could remember when Desmond did not reciprocate the gestures of Douglas. Melvin noted that neither of the two ever wanted for anything while they were in each other's presence, which was most all of the time.

Melvin begrudgingly relented and yielded to Douglas' wishes.

Clearly, Desmond's words had cut deeply into Melvin's mind, spirit, and heart. Yet, however, deep the cut and however harsh the words, they were indeed true! Melvin thought about the fact that during the last three months of his relationship with Julian, he only received telephone calls to discuss some great matter that Julian had participated in or was thinking about entering. The telephone conversations began to become a discussion of nothing more than new political strategies, political rallies, or political debates. Sex between Melvin and Julian had dwindled down to nothing by their sixth month together until Melvin had insisted on some type of sex. In an effort to satisfy his desires, Julian scheduled the sex between them for once a month on the anniversary of their meeting. Although Melvin desperately tried to believe that Julian was still interested in him, he knew that the relationship that had begun passionately and hot was, like the school year, coming to an end.

Xavier, on the other hand, had "dismissed" the good Reverend William Barnes soon after Desmond's confession.

"I'm not a door mat," Xavier told William one Sunday night after dinner. "I have needs too, you know!"

The good Reverend William Barnes did not accept being "dismissed" as easily as Xavier had anticipated it. William actually decided to do everything within his power to keep Xavier and not begin to try to make him happy. As a result, William began to appear unexpectedly in Jackson more often.

On one evening a few weeks before the end of the semester, Melvin noticed William leaving their dorm room in a rage.

"What did you do to him?" Melvin asked as the door almost slammed off of the hinges. "He looks pretty stirred up about something or the other."

"I'm sick of his shit, honey," Xavier grumbled. "And I told him as much! Hell, I want to eat at *Madison's* sometimes rather than at *McDonald's* all of the damned time! So, I told him to keep his broke ass in Memphis!"

"Guhl," Melvin said in astonishment. "I wouldn't ever dare consider telling Julian some crazy shit like that! Have you lost your damned mind?"

"Yes, I have lost my damned mind, Melvin," Xavier exclaimed. "After I thought about what I missed out on by loosing Desmond, I had to do an inventory of my life. Look at how Douglas adores Desmond! Look at how they treat one another with respect. They are so in love until it is almost sickening and worse yet, they actually love one another and it's not all about the fireball sex. So, I told William to get his ass in gear or be prepared to be kicked to the curb! Furthermore, you need to stop being Julian's door mat!"

"Do you ever get tired of all of the running around that you have to do with William?" Melvin asked as he thought about his own situation.

"Child," Xavier chuckled. "Actually I do! You know that I love traveling around the countryside and using my god given talents!"

"I'm assuming that you are talking about your voice," Melvin teased. "You know that you can tear a church up, honey. Now these other talents, I don't know anything about."

"I'm talking about my voice, hooker," Xavier laughed. "I truly can actually thank William for one major contribution that he has made to this relationship. He introduced me to people that I would have never met by myself. Because of him, I have not only met some great musicians but I have also met some of the most popular gospel recording artists in the business. Hopefully, by next year, I am going to release my first album!"

"You've already made an album," Melvin questioned.

"Not yet," Xavier explained. "William and I travel to Grenada, Mississippi a lot of weekends and I have laid a few tracks down at his uncle's studio."

"So that's why you don't mind traveling with him, heffa," Melvin laughed. "You are getting something out of it too!"

"Well, he's getting something out of me," Xavier laughed. "Until he can make up his mind whether or not he is gay, what am I supposed to do, just wait on him?"

"Well," Melvin commented. "I am somewhat waiting on Julian's career but I am also laying the foundations for my own."

"Well," Xavier giggled as he threw his legs into the air to illustrate his sexual prowess. "I truly can say that I get joy when I think about what William does to me. Damn, the dick is good, guhl!"

Melvin laughed and then threw a pillow at Xavier.

Xavier caught the pillow and threw it back at Melvin.

Chapter Nine
Since I Laid My Burdens Down

Come, ye disconsolate
Wherever ye languish!
Come to the mercy seat.
Fervently kneel!
Here bring your wounded heart!
Here tell your anguish!
Earth has no sorrow
That Heaven cannot heal

Melvin slipped slightly into depression after the death of his grandfather in 1993. Death had always been an intricate part of his life as he was the child of a mortician. Nevertheless, Melvin felt that he had become immune to the affects of death and dying yet he was not immune to pain and suffering within life.

In the final months of Jeremiah Hanks's life, Melvin temporarily withdrew from Lane College in order to care for him. Melvin could not bear the thought of allowing his grandfather to be placed in a nursing facility within Dyer County. Although there were several good facilities in Dyer County to place the elderly who needed care, Melvin would not allow his grandfather to be removed from the confines of his own home as the twilight years rolled on his life.

To Melvin's amazement, Julian had been very supportive of his decision to temporarily withdraw from school in order to care for his grandfather. Melvin loved him deeper because of his concern. Melvin realized that his relationship with Julian was not the best one in the world yet he also realized that unlike so many other people, he still had a relationship. Although affection had totally left the relationship, Melvin remained in it.

"Why do you torture yourself, Melvin?" Bradley questioned one in a telephone conversation. "You know you deserve better than him!"

"I'm satisfied with him," Melvin lied.

"Satisfies with what?" Bradley yelled. "Is sex once a month satisfying to you?"

"I have sex more than once a month," Melvin lied again.

The truth of the matter was that Melvin chose not to have sex with Julian anymore because there was no intimacy left between them. The passion and romance had dissolved. By the time Melvin had decided to withdraw from Lane College, the only sex that Melvin and Julian had occurred occasionally when Julian wanted a quick blow job during the week or on their monthly anniversary meeting. Melvin had come to despise the monthly meeting because it seemed to be more of a chore rather than the original passion that he once shared with Julian.

"Child," Bradley blurted out. "I've got some tea for you!"

Melvin welcomed the change of subject because he enjoyed hearing good gossip.

"Tell, tell," Melvin said eagerly.

"When have you heard from your Uncle Claiborne?" Bradley asked.

"He sent me a leather trench coat for Christmas," Melvin explained. "It was lovely because he also sent the matching hat, gloves, and briefcase. I think that it was *Louis Vetton*. Why?"

"Have you seen his latest video?" Bradley asked.

"What video?"

"Oh shit," Bradley said. "You don't know!"

"I don't know what?"

"Your uncle is one of the biggest porn stars in the business right now," Bradley informed.

Melvin was speechless as Bradley continued his litany. When Bradley completed his very graphic and detailed story, he asked: "You mean you didn't know?"

"I live in Tennessee," Melvin said. "He lives in Georgia. How in the hell would I know that?"

"He does not live here," Bradley said. "He only owns a bar here. He actually lives in New York."

"This is too much for me to handle right now," Melvin said in disgust. "When will you be home?"

"I'm moving back next month," Bradley informed.

"What?" Melvin asked.

"I'm moving home next month," Bradley repeated. "I'm tired of the rat race and need some peace and quiet and RoEllen is just the place to get that."

"Are you in trouble or something?" Melvin asked because he knew that Bradley, for as far as he could remember, hated the country life and country living.

"No, I'm not in trouble," Bradley stated firmly.

"Well," Melvin asked. "What brought this on then?"

"I just need to get the hell away from Atlanta for a minute," Bradley confessed. "I finally did the relationship thing! Unfortunately, it did not work out. So, I just need a change of pace for the minute. You know; something slow, where I can just clear my thoughts and get my head together."

"Why didn't you ever tell me that you were in a relationship Bradley Kelly?" Melvin quizzed.

"Because you never asked," Bradley replied. "Every time we talked you were talking about what you and Julian were planning."

"Touché," Melvin laughed. "Are you gonna stay with your mother or what?"

"Hell no," Bradley said. "I own a patch of land in RoEllen. One of the agreements that I made with my ex is that he had to buy me a doublewide trailer to put on it if I agreed to leave without making his life totally more miserable than it already was. So, I'm putting it up on my land next door to where my Uncle Bee Bop used to live."

"He bought you a double wide trailer?" Melvin asked in awe.

"I don't date paupers, honey," Bradley laughed. "He would have had a house built but that would have kept me in Atlanta for an extra year and he was trying to get me totally and completely out of his hair."

"And obviously out of his pocket book," Melvin teased.

"Especially out of that," Bradley laughed. "How is the gang doing anyway? I haven't heard from anyone in a while?"

"Well," Melvin informed. "Desmond and Douglas just purchased a new townhouse in Jackson. Xavier just signed a new contract with a record label and he is now on tour. Howard just moved back to Dyersburg from Memphis and he is teaching school somewhere in Crocket County. Frederick is still at the nursing home."

"When will Frederick ever do more for himself?" Bradley asked. "He knows that he can do better!"

"Well," Melvin mused. "He is quite content with being half man and half drag queen."

"Has he dressed up yet?" Bradley inquired.

"Well," Melvin explained. "He only gets in drag garb for the weekend. Bradley, he looks hideous too! He has this tired ass wig on, an old red church dress that he got from somebody's trash, and some black pumps that are so run over, I don't see how he manages to ever attempt to walk in them."

"He doesn't go to Memphis like that," Bradley said. "I hope!"

"Naw, child," Melvin laughed. "He performs in the taverns in Dyersburg or Newbern and sometimes he ventures out to Covington or Union City."

"Whatever," Bradley laughed as he tried to imagine the description of Frederick in drag that Melvin had just given him. "I'll see you in a month!"

"I'll be here," Melvin said.

Bradley returned to Tennessee on the day that Jeremiah Hanks had given up the ghost. Bradley knew that something was terribly wrong when he pulled his 1992 *Toyota Camry* into the driveway of Melvin's beloved Gramps Jeremiah. Cars had lined the street and there was not an available parking spot in the driveway. He hurriedly parked his car, ran into the house, greeting mourners as he sifted through the crowd in search of his friend. Finally he found Melvin on the back porch.

Melvin, in an attempt to try to collect his thoughts, had decided that this would be the only place on his grandfather's land that would afford him some peace.

"Come on," Bradley said as he approached Melvin. "We need to go for a ride!"

"Bradley," Melvin managed to choke out in a whisper as tears streamed from his eyes. "Gramps is gone!"

Bradley said nothing.

He immediately grabbed Melvin and hugged him.

Melvin cried in the arms of his best friend for what seemed to be an eternity. Upon completion of his teary moment, Bradley managed to sift back through the crowd with Melvin in tow. He managed to usher Melvin to his *Camry* and began to drive away from the house of mourning, the crowd, and the present dilemma.

"I want to go to Jackson," Melvin finally managed to say to Bradley after they had driven a few blocks away from the house of mourning. "I want to see Julian."

"You got it," Bradley said as he drove westward down Highway 104 until he reached his turn off on Highway 412- South which would lead them to Jackson, Tennessee from Dyer County.

Melvin said nothing during the trip.

Bradley did not require him to say anything either. Instead, Bradley turned the radio onto Jackson's *Kix 96* and listened to music. By the grace of God, the music was uplifting. Bradley did not want to hear downtrodden ballads at this particular moment.

Upon entering Jackson, Melvin directed Bradley to Julian's apartment complex.

They pulled into the apartment complex and searched for a parking space near Julian's shining 1993 *Buick LeSabre.*

Melvin had a strange feeling. He shrugged it off as his nerves just being unsettled due to the death of his grandfather.

Melvin reached into his pocket and retrieved the key that Julian had given him for emergency purposes only.

Bradley followed closely behind Melvin as Melvin walked quickly to the apartment.

The music Luther Vandross could be heard playing loudly.

It was coming from Julian's apartment.

Melvin opened the door and walked in with Bradley directly behind him. Melvin noticed a bottle of wine and a half empty wine glass on the coffee table. This was not uncommon for Julian.

Melvin looked into the kitchen and noticed that there was food on the countertop that had obviously been recently purchased. This did not unnerve him as Julian often brought food home to eat and would leave it on the countertop before eating.

Melvin decided against calling Julian's name because he wanted to just speak to him in person.

Melvin, felt that because the music was so loud that it was very possible that Julian was in the bathroom.

He walked to the bathroom and there was no one in it.

He opened Julian's bedroom door and walked into the room and turned the light on.

Melvin's mind registered but did not register the sight that he saw.

Julian was in bed with a woman!

"JULIAN!" Melvin managed to yell which caused Julian to turn around in shock.

The startled young lady was actually beautiful! Her skin was a creamy yet light brown. Her hair was, although somewhat out of place, long and well managed. Her manicured fingers that stretched forth onto Julian's back were painted a soft pink.

"Oh, I'm sorry for interrupting," Melvin gasped as he took a step backward, turned the lights back out, and exited the bedroom.

"Wait!" Julian said as he jumped out of the bed, ran to the door, flung it opened wide, and ran to Melvin who was quickly walking out of the door followed by Bradley.

"Explain!" Melvin said as he turned around quickly and looked into Julian's eyes. "There is nothing to explain!"

"Yes there is!" Julian pleaded.

Melvin grabbed Julian's organ and squeezed hard.

"It's still hard, Julian," Melvin growled. "Go on back in there and get your nut!"

Melvin released Julian's organ.

Julian began to knuckle forward.

Melvin turned and proceeded to walk out of the apartment. Before he opened the front door, however, he looked at Julian and with all of the strength that he could muster, threw Julian's keys toward his face.

The keys flowed through the air but missed the target they were aimed for.

"Fuck you, man," Melvin managed as tears rushed down his face almost blinding him as he ran frantically toward Bradley's car. Bradley ran and opened the door for him. He sat in the car and Bradley sat beside him.

"Just drive," Melvin said as his tears finally subsided. He then stared blankly out of the window.

"You don't need this," Bradley said as he whisked through the streets of Jackson and back to Dyer County. Melvin said nothing.

During the funeral process, Melvin lodged at Bradley's new double wide trailer and gave explicit instructions not to be disturbed by anyone. Fortunately, the process only took three days and the funeral was set.

At the funeral, Melvin chose to sit on the second pew directly behind his mother. Bradley sat on his right and Desmond sat on his left. Xavier, accompanied by Howard, sang a very moving *I'll Fly Away* which of course moved the crowd. Melvin was present in body only. His mind was millions of miles away. He could not remember anything about the stately funeral or any of the people who had attended.

Melvin was oblivious to his Gramps Jeremiah's casket being lifted by the pallbearers, countless ushers who grabbed and toted floral spray after floral spray after floral spray, or when Bradley and Desmond escorted him to the graveyard that was located a few feet from the church.

As he prepared to join his family underneath the tent that had been placed by James Funeral Home over the freshly dug grave, Julian managed to stop him.

"Melvin," Julian began. "You just don't understand…"

Melvin looked at Julian as if he had never seen him before.

"How dare you bring this bullshit to my grandfather's burial," Melvin raged through clinched teeth yet lowered voice. He certainly did not want to bring any more attention to himself and certainly did not want this conversation heard by anyone.

"I've been trying to contact you ever since I found out about your grandfather dying…" Julian attempted to explain.

"I have been unavailable at my request due to bereavement," Melvin said shortly.

"Melvin," a familiar voice called from about two feet away. "I'm terribly sorry for your loss. If there is anything that I can do, just let me know."

The voice moved in closer to him. Melvin realized that Bradley and Douglas had moved slightly away from him as this voice came closer but had been tightly beside him while Julian spoke to him. The voice immediately calmed his spirit. When he managed to look up at the six foot two inch framed man who was meticulously dressed in a tailored black suit, polished shoes, a starched white shirt with a monogram on the collar, and an expensive tie ensemble Melvin did not know whether to smile, laugh, cry, or scream.

It was The Rev.

"Thank you so much for coming," Melvin said as he placed his hand into The Rev's large hand as tears began to flow from his cheeks. The Rev instantly hugged him.

Julian grabbed The Rev's shoulder.

"Oh wait a minute," Julian began.

"I advise you to get your hands off of me, Mr. Jordan," The Rev warned.

"And who the hell are you?" Julian questioned in rage.

Melvin quickly gained his composure and twisted out of the grasp and comfort of The Rev's hug. He had to stop an ensuing brawl. He knew The Rev could have a hot temper and if The Rev's temper flared, he normally would forget where he was. Melvin also knew that Julian's temper could match The Rev's given the opportunity. Fortunately, however, Bradley, Desmond, Douglas, Howard, Xavier and even Frederick were there to save the day.

"Gentlemen," Bradley whispered. "We are in the cemetery at the burial of the dead. Have you no ethics? Julian, could you please leave?"

"Why do I have to go?" Julian whispered angrily.

"Because you are in danger," Bradley grinned. "I don't mind..."

"I just want to be alone with my frat brothers, if you don't mind, Julian," Melvin stated firmly. He also knew the look on Bradley's face. Bradley, a typical Kelly, was in fight mode and the last thing that Melvin needed was a fight at the gravesite of his beloved grandfather.

Fortunately, Julian respected Melvin's request and walked a short distance away from the burial.

As Gramps Jeremiah Hanks's body was lowered into the ground beside his beloved Bertha in the Mt. Carmel Baptist Church Cemetery in Fairhaven, Tennessee, one of the elderly deacons began to lead the assembled congregation into one of Gramps Jeremiah's favorite tunes.

Glory, glory!

Hallelujah!

Since I laid my burdens down!

Glory, glory!

Hallelujah!

Sine I laid my burdens down!

Melvin had chosen not to sit down with the rest of his family who were seated beside the open grave with the casket that sat on top waiting to be "committed to the ground" by the minister. He stood somewhat behind the tent as the pageantry of rural southern funeral rites continued. The Rev placed a warm yet firm hold around Melvin's waist. For a brief moment, Melvin felt safely in love in the arms of one of the men who had always been an inspiration in his life. Somehow, his strength began to return as he stood in The Rev's arms, the minister committed the body to the ground, and then a member of James Funeral Home thanked the people for their support and then dismissed the assembly.

The crowd dispersed from the gravesite and descended on the fellowship hall of Mt. Carmel to eat a scrumptious meal prepared by the members of the community. Melvin chose this time to find Julian and lead him a distance into the cemetery away from the hearing of the mourners.

"I don't understand you," Melvin stated firmly. "Nor will I forgive you anytime soon!"

"Please don't be this way," Julian said.

Melvin looked at Julian as if for the first time ever.

"Why?" Melvin asked as he began to thoroughly loath Julian within his heart.

"She's my fiancée," Julian said.

Like Anita once sang *No more tears for you* Melvin no longer had any for Julian.

"When in the fuck did you become a straight man?" Melvin asked.

"I've got to have a wife," Julian said. "Melvin, you know that my career depends on it."

Melvin rolled his eyes as Julian. At that moment, Melvin literally began to hate Julian and everything that Julian stood. The countless conversations the two had over liberation of humanity flooded Melvin's memory.

"We've been engaged for over a year," Julian confessed.

The sting of this new truth and revelation was more than Melvin could handle at the moment.

Melvin slapped Julian. The lick was so hard until it left a bruise on Julian's face.

"I deserve that," Julian said as he held his face.

"Why in the hell did you string me along?" Melvin asked as fury began to swell within him.

"I just wanted to see what it was like," Julian said casually. "It was good. I enjoyed it."

"Well," Melvin grumbled. "I hope the hell that you enjoyed it while it lasted."

"I'm sorry if I hurt you," Julian said.

"I'm beyond hurt, anymore," Melvin said. "Julian, I once believed in you. The only thing that I know, though, is that I am a black gay man who needs another black gay man in his life. I don't need anybody who is confused or have to hide in order to love me."

"Why was that tall guy touching you?" Julian asked.

"What difference does it make?" Melvin said.

"I still want you!" Julian said.

Melvin was floored.

"Want me?" Melvin asked. "You want me! You just told me that you have a fiancée. You couldn't possibly want me because in case you have forgotten, I am not a woman and I do not do drag!"

"I still want you!" Julian insisted.

"Baby, just as we have laid Gramps Jeremiah down," Melvin smirked. "You laid our relationship down for some pussy! So, I too am going to lay this burden down right now!"

"No, baby…" Julian said.

"Julian," Melvin stated firmly. "I never want to see or hear from you again!"

"But," Julian said as he attempted to embrace Melvin.

Melvin quickly stepped away from his grasp.

"You heard him," Bradley said. "Now, Mr. Julian Jordan, it's time for you to go!"

Julian looked up and realized that he stared into the faces of The Rev, Bradley, Howard, Frederick, Desmond, Douglas and Xavier. A great look of disgust appeared on his face.

He chose to walk away, however, because he knew that if he risked getting into an altercation with members of the Alumni Association of Omega Phi Theta at the gravesite of one of its member's loved ones, he would have a terrible price to pay for it. Politically, it would ruin him for certainly the rumor would some leak out that he was fighting over a gay man.

Julian stared in contempt at the group once again.

He looked one final time at Melvin in hopes that there was a slight glimmer of forgiveness.

The look that Melvin returned said it all.

Julian yielded and walked away sorrowfully.

Chapter Ten

Making Preparations: 1997

When you hear of my home going,
Don't worry 'bout me!
When you hear of my home Going
Don't worry 'bout me!
When you hear of my home Going
Don't worry 'bout me!
I'm just another soldier
On my way home!

As the new millennium slowly approached, life in Dyer County began to change. Melvin, Bradley, Howard, Desmond, and Frederick had begun to grow older and the wonderful years of their twenties were quickly coming to an end. Yet, the new millennium had yet arrived.

Frederick traveled to *Desmond Beauty and Barber Shop* in Jackson, Tennessee in order to get his hair "fixed" for one of the greatest events that would occur in his life up to this point. After years of labor and personal turmoil, he finally made the decision to participate in his first "drag show" at *The Apartment Club* in Memphis, Tennessee. *The Apartment Club* was hosting its final pageant before it closed its doors and Frederick wanted to be a part of the historic event.

Slowly over the years Frederick had yielded to an inner transformation and calling. He could not understand this demon yet it constantly tugged and raged a war within him. No one could understand why he could not explain this tug at his spirit. However, the glamour and beauty of seeing himself dressed in women's clothing and looking like a women consumed him. He had long ago distanced himself from the abuse that he had endured within his family. Hence, there was no one except his immediate friends that he could seek acceptance from within the ever changing world. For years, he had hidden this great secret from them until he could bear it no further.

In the early part of the decade of the 1990s, many black gay men who lived in the rural south attended talent shows hosted at local taverns in their home towns dressed in drag. Because it was an entertaining matter to the inhabitants, it was allowed and welcomed. Hence, many a drag queen won the talent shows dressed as closely as was possible to the style and glamour found within the drag queens that lived in the metropolitan areas. Some could not remain in the small towns and moved on to the metropolis where an entirely new and different life willingly waited for them. Frederick was no stranger to the life of a rural drag queen. When finally he learned how to dress properly in drag, he entered talent shows in taverns or juke joints as well. He managed to even win a few in Dyersburg, Newbern, Fairhaven, Covington, or even Union City. He dared not even compete with Memphians because the competition there was far too heavy for him. The legends of the day had stamped the drag communities with their own identities and had begun to form Families and houses bearing their names whereas young and forthcoming drag queens would flock to become part of the culture. Because Frederick was getting older, he decided against joining or even being associated with a gay Family or House and instead settled with being *Alexis LaBelle Houston* when he performed. His name had derived from three women that he admired the most... Alexis Morel Carrington Colby Dexter Rowe from *Dynasty*, Patti LaBelle, and Whitney Houston.

But, 1997 had come and the closing of *The Apartment Club* was in town for West Tennessee. Although Frederick never dressed in drag in Memphis because he could not afford to dress as elegantly as the legendary drag queens, his desire to be a participant in the last pageant at *The Apartment Club* grew so great until he could not resist entering the pageant. When he first announced that he was going to enter the *1997 Miss Black Gay West Tennessee Pageant* sponsored by the legends of *The Apartment Club*, his circle of friends were shocked. They all knew that he occasionally dressed in drag and performed in the rural taverns but they questioned Frederick's ability to pull off such a great feat among the Memphis drag queens that would definitely show the upcoming drag queens the ropes at winning a pageant.

"Child, if you are going to compete," Bradley confided. "We are going to make sure that you represent these guhls well who are from the sticks!"

Bradley took Frederick's body measurements as they would be in drag. He then called fashion designers that he had met from Atlanta, New York, and Chicago and asked them to send him patterns and designs that would fit the measurements that he had sent to them. Because Frederick was short, some of the patterns that Bradley received would have been difficult to achieve the sleek and unique look that Bradley felt Frederick needed in order to pull of this new quest. Frederick did have the waist line for most of the patterns that Bradley received which gave him endless opportunity.

After Bradley and Frederick discussed, argued, and finally compromised on three gowns that could be worn, Bradley ordered fabric from New York, London, and Paris. Frederick's eyes watered when the fabric arrived and Bradley showed him the lace that would be used to sew the dress for Frederick's performance of Stephanie Mill's *Home* which would be a tribute to his now deceased friend, Vincien.

In 1995, Frederick had cried for weeks upon hearing the news of Vincien's death. Vincien had died of complications from AIDS. Vincien was the first person in Frederick's life that had not been from Dyer County that he had befriended. Frederick had considered Vincien as his gay role model, his gay mother, and his gay father. Vincien had attempted to teach Frederick how to truly love himself and as a result Frederick began to embrace himself and not fear what the world might think of him. After Vincien's death, however, Frederick because of depression, became a recluse and seldom left his house except to go to work and return to it. It was Bradley and Melvin who insisted that Frederick snap out of his depression, *"fluff back up, beat his face into place, and jump back into the race"* as Patti LaBelle advises.

Upon entering back "into the race", Frederick decided that he would do drag completely on the weekends. At first, he looked ridiculous but as time passed by, he began to hone his craft. In the beginning, he was ridiculed by many people but as time gradually passed along, he became accepted by society when people realized that he was going to wear women's clothes whether it was liked or not.

Bradley uncovered the deepest most beautiful shade of blue velvet that would be used for Frederick's second act during the pageant. In this act, Frederick would wear a chicly fashioned fitted the two pieced velvet suit with an over exaggerated matching blue hat that had wide plumes stretching high into the air while a thin layer of white fur would trim it. The sleeves and collar of the suit would be trimmed in white fur. The skirt to the suit would be three-quarter in length with a split down the side of the right leg. This would offer the viewer a chance to see the matching velvet shoes that were also trimmed in fur. During the performance, light gospel music would be played as Frederick would stand at a podium and read James Weldon Johnson's poem *The Creation*. At the finale of the poem when Frederick was scheduled to say *"And man became a living soul,"* he would unveil a white sheet that had covered a fine, black man, who was drenched in muscles.

Frederick felt that several men could easily play the role well but none could play it quite as good as his ex-lover Garrett. Garrett and Frederick had briefly dated before Vincien died in 1995. Frederick had only dated Garrett because of how he made him look. Garrett was indeed an uncouth "rough neck" from a suburb of Memphis, Tennessee known as Orange Mound. He had recently been released from *Fort Pillow Prison* in Henning, Tennessee. He and Frederick had corresponded through letters for three months prior to his releases. Physically, he was above and beyond Frederick's expectations. Frederick, like most black gay men, was in love with manly looking men and Garrett was a man's man by any standard. He stood six feet three inches and weighed two hundred and thirty pounds and every pound was a muscle. His hands resembled bear paws and his legs, to Frederick, looked like the legs of a giant. His manhood easily measured eleven inches. He had a gold tooth on his front tooth that was displayed when he laughed. His voice was deep and rich, almost sounding like thunder when he spoke. Garrett was a natural hustler yet his hustles, in Frederick's opinion, were always considered weak or stupid. When together, his mere presence made Frederick appear womanly which added to Frederick's reasons for dating him. After a month of freedom, the lack of finding reasonable employment due to a lack of education and a lack of employment history, he began his feeble hustles again. His hustles unfortunately included sleeping with men for money. Frederick would not stand for it and ended the relationship yet not the occasional moments of exciting sex with him for a few dollars, of course. Two years later, he had developed more muscles, so, Frederick agreed to give him $50 to sit under the sheet without anything on except a thong during the performance. He was thoroughly instructed by Frederick to stand when the sheet was removed. Secretly, Frederick offered Garrett an extra $40 to escort him from the pageant home. The amenities would be a great round of sex with someone he knew, breakfast and lunch, and then a bus ticket back to Memphis the following day.

Frederick literally fell backward when Bradley opened the box containing the material that would be used for the gown to be worn for his final performance.

"How much money did you spend for this?" Frederick asked Bradley as he gawked at the hot pink sequin trimmed in golden beads that held rhinestone, rubies, and pearls.

"Someone owed me a favor," Bradley laughed. "I thought that you would look perfect in this when they crown you."

When Desmond had learned that Frederick was entering the pageant and that Bradley was creating the dresses, he insisted that Frederick come to his main salon in Jackson to get his hair fixed.

"You need a French roll and a freeze, child," Desmond said as Frederick sat in the chair patiently awaiting the assault Desmond would soon give his hair. Although Desmond was an excellent beautician, he was extremely heavy handed.

Heavy handed or not, Frederick trusted only Desmond on his head.

Hence, Desmond styled Frederick's hair whereas he could easily manage it and still change with the varying scenes of the pageant. The scene changes would mean changes in hair as well, so, Desmond styled four different wigs for Frederick for the event.

Melvin became engrossed in the activity as well. He simply could not allow Bradley and Desmond to show him up. Melvin called his Uncle Claiborne and explained the situation. He needed a shipment of make-up that would not run but would be perfect for a drag show.

"You are not doing drag now are you?" Uncle Claiborne asked.

"Heavens no," Melvin laughed. "One of my best friends recently entered a pageant in Memphis and we are trying to make sure that he gets the crown because, after all, he is representing us!"

"I'll over night it to you then," Uncle Claiborne laughed. "He may need to try out the different shades and colors. I will send him a rejuvenating treatment along with it. But it will stand up to the lights for hours!"

"Thanks, Uncle," Melvin laughed.

Prior to a trip to New Orleans, Xavier consorted with Bradley and took swatches of the material with him. Upon his return, Frederick had shoes in the exact color of each of his changes of clothes for the evening.

The night before the pageant, Melvin hosted a dinner party at his house for the entire gang. He felt that it had been long overdue for the entire group to get together. He was happy that this meeting was not a sad occasion but a happy one.

Desmond, Douglas, and Frederick arrive first.

Melvin hugged each of them as they entered his home.

"Look who I drug up, children," Bradley laughed as he produced Howard.

Melvin laughed and hugged Howard and welcomed him into his home. When Bradley entered, however, he pulled Bradley's ear slightly and then hugged him as well.

"What did you do that for?" Bradley squealed as he attempted to pull out of Melvin's grasp.

"I like Howard and all, Bradley," Melvin whispered. "But the party is in honor of Frederick and you know that they had a really ugly break up years ago!"

"Boy, that was so long ago and so very many men ago," Frederick chuckled and then hugged Howard. "You leave my seamstress alone, honey. He can bring whomever he wishes to a party in my honor!"

Xavier and William came last.

Xavier wore a markedly unhappy expression on his face.

Bradley served appetizers and wine while Melvin put the finishing touches on dinner.

"Child, you laid it out, didn't you?" Desmond laughed as he withdrew a stuffed mushroom from its platter and placed it on a small plate. Melvin had gone the extra mile for the party. He had appetizers of stuffed mushrooms, Rumaki, and smoked salmon on rye. There was also fresh fruit and fruit dip strategically set around the great room for the comfort of the guests. Champagne punch and an assortment of wine chilled in the bar.

The event was impressive, even by Melvin's own standards. He almost could not believe that his journey had led him back to Fairhaven. Yet it had. After he graduated Lane College, he applied as a teller in a bank in Fairhaven. He had only planned to work at the bank for the summer before he was going to move to Nashville, Tennessee. His grandfather's estate came out of escrow which meant that he now owned his own home. Hence, he renovated the house and remained in Fairhaven.

The evening began to fill with laughter as the group began to reminiscence on events that had occurred in the past. Those who had been members of the Omega Phi Theta Fraternity laughed about days in the fraternity. When Howard shared encounters that he had down through the years, Frederick would match them with encounters he had. Somehow, the telling of Frederick's stories were always more vivacious and hilarious.

"You know," Frederick said as he sipped a glass of champagne punch. "If we can all just get together sometimes, what a difference we could make in this neck of the woods!"

"Wouldn't that be a nice thing," Xavier said with a melancholy expression on his face. Xavier thought about life before William and the Gospel Recording Industry. Yes, Xavier had successfully produced three records that had made the top ten lists in gospel music in America. He had also won several *Dove Awards*. He once said that his voice would carry him places and it certainly had.

William now pastored a huge congregation in Memphis. No one seemed to notice or even care when he and Xavier finally moved into a huge house together in Memphis.

Douglas was no the owner or a pizza franchise. Melvin smiled when he thought about when Douglas left school to become a manager. On this salary, however, Douglas still managed to provide Desmond with everything Desmond could ever dream of.

Desmond went on to graduate from *McCollum and Ross* and then pass his state board exam in order to become a licensed cosmetologist. He owned two beauty shops. He took over his Aunt Flora's shop in Newbern and then opened a shop in Jackson.

As a couple, Desmond and Douglas purchased a three bedroom home in north Jackson. The home had a two car garage and a swimming pool.

Howard had moved back to Dyersburg. He was a successful history teacher in Crocket County.

Bradley, when he worked, worked through a temporary agency at various local factories in Dyer County whenever he needed quick money. His primary source of income, however, was the residual he received from stocks that he owned in several Fortune 500 companies that were thriving. Bradley had surprised Melvin when he explained that back in high school he had been advised to invest money into companies like *IBM, Microsoft, Coca-Cola, Wal-Mart,* and

McDonalds. He did this along with insisting that his former three lovers purchase multiple shares of stocks in several companies in his name which they did. They also purchased him countless CDs. Each company's stock that Bradley had chosen to invest in besides the aforementioned soared which only provided him with a very comfortable life in Tennessee. Because of the time that he had on hand, he added an additional room built on to his trailer, installed the latest sewing equipment, and opened a shop whereas he sewed for the public.

"I may not have attended The Art Institute," he would comment. "But I hung out with enough divas in the fashion industry who taught me all of the tricks of the trade."

Subsequently, he was always swamped with work to do for the public.

Melvin served dinner in his newly renovated dining room. His menu included Brajole, carrots and peas, herb fried zucchini, and hot buttered rolls.

A happy yet festive atmosphere loomed over the place as the friends enjoyed the company of each other. It had been quite some time since they had all gotten together. Melvin was elated that over time, he came to accept Frederick for being who Frederick was. Sometimes he would never be able to understand him yet that was the important thing about learning the people in whom you consider your friends.

Soon, the night grew old and most had obligations for the next day. Hence, as they had come, they were inclined to leave. They all wished Frederick success on his performance scheduled for the next night. Xavier and William had to decline attending the performance due to a prior engagement. Douglas also could not attend because of a conflict within his schedule. Desmond, on the other hand would be there.

When all but Frederick, Melvin and Bradley were left, Frederick began to speak more freely.

"You know, Melvin," he began. "I used to not like you because I thought that you tried to be bourgeoisie but when I got to know you, I really came to love you."

Melvin walked to the sofa that he sat on and gave him a huge hug.

"Get used to me, child," Melvin laughed because his feelings had been mutual for Frederick yet he never considered Frederick as being bourgeoisie but rather uncouth instead.

"Yeah," Frederick laughed. "I know you have your ways just like I have mine."

"We all have crazy ways," Bradley interjected and then hugged both of them.

"I wonder why we gay people are not close to one another in these small towns?" Frederick asked. "We live a life time around each other and then try to act like we don't know one another sometimes. We should be much closer than these guhls who live in the city because we have been around each other for so long but we are not! Why is that?"

Melvin escorted Frederick and Bradley to a screened porch where they all sat in seats adjacent to one another. For convenience, Melvin rolled a glass bar onto the porch.

"Well, in the city, you can easily choose who you wish to be around," Bradley said. "You have a choice in deciding who you wish to be your friends and who you wish to be your enemies. In the city, you can easily hang out with the haves and just as easily hang out with the have nots. You pick and choose I the city. You don't have that luxury in the country."

"That's true," Melvin agreed. "You know, I actually love to watch a good drag show but I never thought in a million years that one of my best friends would actually be a drag queen!"

"Female impersonator," Frederick teased. "Thank you very much!"

"When I truthfully look back down through the years, I once thought that because of Melvin's family, he would automatically have to be stuck up," Bradley confessed as he poured himself a rum and Coke. "I never dreamed back then that we would become best friends. But we did. I've always thought you were just crazy as hell, Fred."

"Lord," Frederick giggled. "Ain't nobody called me Fred in years. Child, we are beginning to tell our ages."

"Shit," Melvin laughed. "Ain't nothing old on me period. Nothing gets old but clothes and then you give them to the *Salvation Army*."

"I hear you," Frederick giggled as he refilled his glass of gin and juice. "All I know is that I want to die young and beautiful."

"Why in the hell did you go there?" Bradley asked.

"I don't know," Frederick said. "That's just how I want to go. I want to be young and beautiful where they won't have to do a lot of work on my body when they roll me into the funeral home."

"Child, it's time for me to drive you home, honey" Bradley laughed. "You sound like you are getting a little tipsy."

Frederick did not refuse the offer.

Melvin escorted them to the front lawn and bid them good evening.

Chapter Eleven

How Deep Is Your Love?

Arrayed in glorious grace,
Shall these vile bodies shine?
Will every shape and every face
Look heavenly and divine?

Frederick staggered slightly as he entered his small but cozy one bedroom apartment. He shook his head slightly in order to gain his composure. He walked to his closet, opened it up, and took one more look at the gowns that had been made for his performance.

"Absolutely beautiful," he thought to himself as he closed the closet door and then walked into the bathroom. When in the bathroom, he yanked a scarf off a nearby hook and tied his hair down as instructed by Desmond.

Just as he was about to go into his bedroom and pass out, there was a knock at his door.

"Who is it?" he called.

"Psycho," the voice replied.

Psycho was his "trade" friend from Fairhaven. Frederick enjoyed the attention that Psycho gave him at times yet the sex had become minimal in recent years. Generally, it never amounted to much these days with the exception of Frederick occasionally performing oral sex on him in exchange for a few dollars.

"Well, it's been a while since I've been sexed up and he may be worth it tonight, what the hell?" Frederick thought as he allowed the six foot three inch, muscular bodied man to enter his apartment.

Psycho did not win any awards for good looks anymore although he had once been a reasonably attractive man. His teeth were somewhat bucked now and he had a long scar on the right side of his face. His head was shaved bald and his eyebrows almost met in the center of his face. Psycho was a big man who weighed at least 250 pounds yet every pound was solid muscle. He had the body of a professional weight lifter. This always turned Frederick on. Further, Psycho prided himself throughout the community for sporting a twelve inch penis. Although this frightened others away from Psycho, it had always kept Frederick attracted to him even since their first encounters years ago when he did screw Frederick.

"How are you doing tonight?" Psycho asked as walked into the apartment.

"A little tipsy," Frederick admitted. "What brings you around here tonight?"

"I just wanted to come and holla at you," Psycho said and grinned. His grin crooked to the left side of his face which made him look like an injured bird.

"Well," Frederick giggled. "You have done that. Do you wanna beer or something to drink?"

"Yeah," he said.

Frederick ushered him to the kitchen table.

He sat down.

Frederick retrieved a bottle of beer from the refrigerator and passed it to him.

"I keep *Old English 800* here for you because I know that you like it," Frederick lied. He had bought the beer for Garrett's appearance after the pageant.

Psycho smiled the interesting grin again.

"You know what else I like," Psycho grinned and looked downward toward his penis.

"I don't know if I'm up to it tonight," Frederick said. "Plus, I really don't feel like sucking no dick tonight. But if you want to make love to me, that's a different story."

A slight frown appeared on Psycho's face but he did not say a word.

Psycho took the beer and then walked into Frederick's bedroom. Frederick did not follow him immediately because he did not feel that Psycho was serious. For the past two years, whenever Frederick had told him this, Psycho would frown and then leave.

Tonight was different.

Psycho went into the bedroom and began to take his clothes off.

Frederick became apprehensive at Psycho's actions. He did not know exactly what to expect out of this very muscularly fine big man. In order to keep his mind preoccupied, though, Frederick decided to wash what little dishes that he had left in the sink. When this task quickly came to a completion, he began to find small items within the apartment to clean.

"I need a favor too, baby," Psycho said as he pulled his dirt and greased stained t-shirt off exposing his muscular chest to the night air.

"What is it?" Frederick asked as he continued to tidy his apartment and attempt to not look into the bedroom where Psycho was.

"I need to borrow some money," Psycho asked as he sat down on Frederick's bed and began to pull his dried muddy shoes off revealing dirty socks that had many holes in them.

"I won't have any until Monday," Frederick said expecting him to put the clothes that he had just removed back on and then leave after hearing this revelation.

Psycho removed his pants.

Frederick glanced into the bedroom as Psycho removed his surprisingly clean sky blue boxer underwear.

Although Frederick had seen this man naked before, there was something alluring about him on this evening.

"Oh my God in Heaven," Frederick said as his hands began to shake.

Psycho stood up and walked to the middle of the room. His triceps and biceps rippled like a sculptured Roman gladiator. Everything about him was markedly huge. Frederick could not stop staring at this man's full physic. A slight glowing shine appeared on Psycho's bald peanut shaped head as a slight perspiration vaguely appeared. His huge arms, torso, calves and legs reminded Frederick of caramel apples one would buy from a carnival. Indeed they were beautiful enough to gaze at yet tempting enough to eat. Somehow Psycho's features became softer and less overwhelming as he stood in the doorway and began to fondle his massive penis.

All good reasoning left Frederick.

Frederick wanted him!

It had actually been a long time since Frederick had been involved and even longer since a man had made love to him. The feelings that he would never find a man again faded because in his bedroom, right before him, stood a totally naked, semi-fine, masculine, muscular man who wanted him. Although he had scheduled a rendezvous for the next night, Psycho was present at this very moment. However brief or long this would last, Frederick felt that the temporary fix would heal his wounded ego yet provide him with the strength, courage, and emotional stability that he would need in order to win the pageant. Frederick also needed to feel a man's touch, a man's caress, a man's warmth that would give his body what it so badly wanted, desired, and needed.

Although every cell within Frederick's body screamed out in anticipation of this naked man who stood before him, his legs would not take him the mere twelve steps that were necessary to walk across the threshold of his bedroom door which would allow this huge man with the body of a god and the dick of a mule to screw him. Instead, Frederick feebly and weakly held on to a chair that sat at the eating table for support.

As Psycho grinned and continued to stroke his manhood, strength began to slowly stir within Frederick's legs as he incessantly watched Psycho's penis begin to grow monstrously large in his large caramel colored hands.

Passion began to stir within Frederick. *"Perhaps, he is the man that I need in my life. Perhaps this is the man that I can give my heart, my mind, and my soul to! Maybe I can fall in love with him in time!"* Frederick thought as he looked deeply at Psycho. He dearly wanted to love passionately again. He wanted to love someone deeper than he had ever loved Howard although it seemed impossible. Regardless of the few and frequent relationships that Frederick had after his break up with Howard, he always managed to compare the depths of the relationship, passion, romance, and love to that of his relationship with Howard. When Howard left him for another man, Frederick felt worthless and betrayed and never felt that he could be good enough for anyone. Indeed, he was damaged goods. Yet, on this night, none of those emotions mattered anymore as Psycho continued his erotic act and display in the doorway of his bedroom.

"What's wrong?" Psycho asked. "You claim you been wanting it. Well, now is your chance!"

Psycho climbed into Frederick's bed as if it were his own.

"Indeed I have," Frederick thought as he walked passed Psycho into his bedroom, quickly pulled off his clothes, and then reached to turn the lights off.

"Leave the light on," Psycho said. "I don't care for the dark and I want to see myself."

"Then turn the lamp on beside you," Frederick said as he pointed to a lamp on a night stand beside the bed.

Psycho reached for the lamp and turned the light on.

Frederick turned the ceiling light off.

Psycho's massive body literally filled the entire bed. Frederick, short and petite and only weighing ninety-five pounds slipped his five foot three inch frame into the bed beside the gargantuan that awaited him.

For the first time ever, Psycho pulled Frederick close to him and then kissed him

Passion grew within Frederick as he wrapped his arm around Psycho's thick neck and returned the kiss. At first, Frederick lay atop of Psycho and soon Psycho flipped him over onto his back and continued to kiss him.

Soon, Psycho's kissed became hard and rough.

"Slow down," Frederick panted as Psycho's paws began to maul every inch of his body. Frederick began to feel like Psycho's woman.

"Shut up, bitch!" Psycho groaned as he continued to kiss and lick Frederick.

Frederick complied. He loved for a man to be a man and take charge.

Psycho reached for the lubrication that sat on the night stand and began to rub it across his penis. Frederick reached for it as well yet Psycho's hand prevented him.

Psycho grabbed Frederick by the back of his head and pushed his face forward into the pillow and pulled Frederick's buttocks high into the air. Without warning, Psycho shoved the full length of his penis completely into Frederick.

Frederick could not move!

He could not scream!

He could not do anything.

His breath was completely taken away.

Tears streamed down Frederick's face.

Frederick could not breathe until Psycho withdrew and then began a relentless sexual assault on his body.

When finally Frederick gained control of his breath, Psycho turned him; penis still inside of him, onto his back and without warning began a series of deeply inserted tongue kissing which prevented Frederick from saying anything.

Occasionally, Frederick enjoyed rough, hard, animalistic and bestial sex but he preferred rough sex with someone who had a smaller organ. This had become uncomfortable.

Frederick attempted to push Psycho off of him.

Psycho only grabbed his hands and pushed deeper inside of him.

"Please take it easy," Frederick managed to whimper to no avail as inch by inch Psycho invaded his body.

Frederick attempted to calm himself and relax where he could begin to enjoy Psycho.

"Maybe this won't last long," Frederick thought as Psycho continued to plunge inside of him.

After about an hour of this, Psycho finally slowed down.

Finally, the pain began to subside as Psycho began of litany of long, deep strokes while he began to kiss Frederick.

Finally, Frederick began to return the kisses. His hands began to slide up Psycho's back as he held on for dear life.

"Yeah, baby," Psycho grunted. "Take it all!"

Frederick felt as if someone had begun to attempt pushing a baseball pat into his body. Soon, he began to feel as if nails were grinding inside of his body as Psycho's pace began to quicken again.

Frederick wanted to enjoy this encounter yet the pain was becoming far too great.

Finally, Frederick began to scream in shear agony as tears flowed down his face. He began to pray that this session would soon end!

In order to bring Psycho to climax, Frederick began to sway his hips from side to side.

"Yeah, baby," Psycho whispered in Frederick's ear. "It's been a long time and I'm gonna get this good tonight!"

Frederick felt as if hot coals had been placed inside of him.

He twisted as his eyes began to roll in his head and his voice completely failed.

Suddenly, his body began to accept Psycho's relentless invasion of his body yet the burning sensation would not leave him.

Frederick was too weak to do anything except pray that the man who was on top of him would be sexually satisfied enough to simply leave him alone.

"Where is your wallet," Psycho asked as he began to plunge deeper inside of Frederick. "I need some money for so more stuff."

"I don't have any money," Frederick cried.

It seemed as if Psycho now went ballistic.

He grabbed Frederick by the neck and began to choke him.

Frederick gasped for air and attempted to get away from his now attacker.

"I hate a mothafuckin liar," Psycho said as he grabbed a shoe string that, to Frederick's amazement, was lying on the pillow beside his head.

Psycho slightly released his grip from the gagging Frederick's throat and slipped the shoe string around it.

Psycho then began to pull the shoe string as he brutally began to plunge deeper into Frederick.

"Please don't," Frederick attempted to scream yet only a faint whisper came from between his parted and parched lips.

Tears rolled down his face as he faintly fought Psycho with as much strength as he had left within his body which was not much.

Frederick was too small and became far too tired to fight anymore.

Psycho was extremely large and seemingly his energy began to increase.

Psycho began to pull the shoe strings more.

The pain inside of him grew as Frederick's attempted to wrestle Psycho.

Psycho laughed and plunged deeper and then began to pull the shoe string tighter.

Frederick stopped trying to wrestle Psycho completely.

Frederick now attempted to place his hands between the shoe string and his throat. His eyes began to bulge as he desperately began to fight for a breath of air.

Frederick became frantic.

Psycho began to howl as he began to pull the shoe strings even tighter around a gagging and weeping Frederick's throat.

"God damned, this is good," Psycho yelled as he pulled the shoe strings with all of his might and exploded hot semen within Frederick's body.

Frederick's mind raced backward in time.

Frederick saw Vincien standing on the stage of *The Apartment Club* singing *Home*. Vincien was beautiful. He was dressed in a white gown and a bright light seemed to shine all around him.

He saw fraternity members who had been dead. They were dressed in tuxedos and were on their way to a ball.

He saw former high school peers that had been dead for years on their way to class.

He saw former choir members from Mt. Carmel clad in white robes with golden stoles. They were singing *Oh, Lord have mercy! Oh, Lord have mercy! Oh, Lord have mercy! Have mercy on me!*

He saw his grandmother, Jewel Temple, smiling a warm smile.

"It's over now, baby" she said. *"Come on in the house!"*

Last, he saw a man who looked like B. D. Ickles.

"You can do it," Ickles said. *"Just do it for me!"*

"Why?" Frederick whispered and closed his eyes.

Frederick then saw *The Glorious Light* and gave up the ghost as all life had escaped him with his last words.

Psycho withdrew himself from Frederick.

"That was good, baby," Psycho said. "Now go get yourself cleaned up for daddy, I might want some more!"

Frederick did not move.

His eyes were closed and his head was slightly turned to the side with the shoestrings still around his neck.

"I guess I put you to sleep," Psycho chuckled wickedly.

Psycho went to the bathroom, took a shower, and returned to the bedroom.

Frederick had still not moved.

Psycho decided to get dressed.

Frederick did not move.

Psycho decided that he would search the apartment and find Frederick's wallet before he woke up. He found it on the living room table. Frederick had ninety dollars which Psycho immediately placed in his pocket. Beside the wallet was a gold chain that Psycho also placed in his pocket.

Psycho went to the refrigerator and withdrew a bottle of *Old English 800.* At first he was going to drink it and maybe go and kiss Frederick good night but he changed his mind and decided to leave.

As he left the apartment, he dropped his cigarettes. He picked them up and disappeared into the night.

Chapter Twelve

Young & Beautiful

Awake, my soul: stretch every nerve,
And press with vigor on;
A Heavenly race demands thy zeal,
And an immortal crown.

Melvin began to worry about Frederick. He did not receive a telephone call from him throughout the entire day that followed the dinner party. It seemed as if he had talked to everybody about Frederick on that day but he had not talked to Frederick on the very day of the pageant.

"Have you talked with Frederick today," Melvin questioned Bradley over the telephone at six o'clock that evening.

"No," Bradley said. "I haven't talked to him since I dropped him off last night."

"I called him," Melvin said. "But I only got the answering machine."

"Well he should be at home," Bradley said. "We are supposed to be leaving here at six-thirty or a quarter 'til seven so we can get everything set up before the pageant starts."

"I have had Frederick on my mind all day," Melvin confessed. "Something just doesn't seem right to me."

"You know," Bradley said. "I felt the same way. Oh yeah, Howard is supposed to be going with us tonight. I think he is trying to get back with Frederick on the sly."

"He may be too late," Melvin said.

The wind blew strongly.

A cold, dry, chill befell Melvin as if a ghost had just passed by him.

Melvin met Bradley and Howard at Bradley's trailer in RoEllen.

They exchanged pleasantries before Melvin began his inquiry.

"Has anyone seen or heard from Frederick at all today?" Melvin inquired.

"I haven't" Howard said. "I've been at church most of the day and none of you all came to any of the services this morning or this afternoon at Mt. Carmel."

"I just didn't feel it today?" Melvin confessed.

"I haven't seen him or talked to him since last night when I dropped him off at home," Bradley stated firmly and began to dial Frederick's number. The telephone rang and then the answering machine picked up.

"We need to get over to his apartment," Melvin said. "Something just ain't right."

"I was thinking the same thing," Bradley agreed.

Melvin, Howard, and Bradley drove to Frederick's apartment in Newbern. They decided to ride with Melvin being he had Bradley blocked into his driveway. Melvin drove quickly to Frederick's small apartment in Newbern.

Melvin knocked on the door.

There was no answer.

Bradley began to beat on the door.

There was no answer.

Howard began to beat on the door.

There was no answer.

"Fuck this," Howard said as he turned the doorknob.

To his amazement, the door was not locked.

The three entered the apartment cautiously.

They noticed a half empty bottle of *old English 800* sitting on the kitchen table.

The noticed that there was a light on in Frederick's bedroom.

The telephone rang and the answering machine picked up.

"Frederick," the voice said. "This is Desmond. I can't understand why you won't pick up?"

Howard noticed someone was in Frederick's bed. He walked into the bedroom

"He must've taken a sleeping pill and is still asleep," Howard said as he walked toward Frederick.

Howard touched Frederick.

Frederick did not respond.

Howard began to shake Frederick.

Frederick's eyes opened but he did not wake up.

Howard patted Frederick's face.

He did not wake up.

"He's dead," Bradley said. "Don't touch anything. Dial 911!"

Melvin dialed 911 and then walked outside of the apartment.

There was a foul heavy odor in the air that had begun to take Melvin's breath away.

Soon, Melvin was overwhelmed with grief as tears began to stream down his face.

Frederick died...

young and beautiful!

Chapter Thirteen
Move One Up A Little Higher

The day is past and gone,
The evening shades appear;
Oh, may we all remember well
The night of death draws near.

Melvin watched in disbelief as the paramedics removed Frederick's body from the tiny apartment. Melvin could not believe the sight within the bedroom. The sheets were soiled with blood yet the smell of dried sex was heavy in the air. Although it was an awfully musty and stale smell, it was apparent to Melvin, Bradley, Howard and even the paramedics that brutal sex had occurred in the bedroom.

Melvin could not understand the vicious motif behind Frederick's death.

"Why would anyone want to kill him? Yes, he had a fascinating way of expressing himself but he wasn't a bad person at all! He would literally remove the shirt from his back to give to a person in need. Lord, help me understand this!" Melvin thought

Melvin hugged both Bradley and Howard who seemed consumed by the matter and definitely prostrate with grief. The shock of it all was far too great for Melvin to process at the moment. He had become numb.

Throughout the entire decade of the 1990s, there had been countless, needless, violent and unnecessary deaths within the African American male population of Dyer County. Most of the men who died had been young men all between the ages of twenty and thirty! Unsuspecting assailants had stabbed some men to death. Other men had been shot to death at point-blank range. Other men had been found in cars dead from shots to the head. When that seemed to not be enough, AIDS had slipped into the community and claimed lives as well. The former deaths had been documented as suicides or unsolvable mysteries to the police and sheriff departments. The fraternity Alumni had begun to bury so many brothers until it was no longer a total surprise when death approached the steps of the Omega Complex.

The entire reality frightened Melvin.

He felt that death should be reserved only for the elderly or the terminally ill. Now, it was common place for ministers to preach sermons to people of all ages, begging them to "get right with God" because death was no stranger to any age group.

"When had death ever been a stranger to any group?" Melvin thought. *"What a tragic irony!"*

1990 ushered in a monstrous yet disastrous change in rural West Tennessee. Young African Americans had begun to flee the nostalgic way of life that the rural south offered. They preferred the chaotic life depicted on television and had began a feeble replication of what they saw. The invention of "crack cocaine" made its way to the South by the middle and ending of the 1980s. Crack hit the south like a hurricane or cyclone. The drug managed to affect the lives of every African American individual within the rural south in some way or another. Young African American males seemed to be affected by it the greatest. Street corners where legendary "whine-Os" formally hung out were replaced with young men attempting to make the infamous "drug deals." Families were utterly destroyed by husbands, wives, fathers, mothers, sons, daughters, brothers, sisters or cousins who had become either a drug addict or a drug dealer. The new community hymn of "supply and demand" replaced the old community hymn of "community and education".

An entire pay check could easily be spent at a "crack house" if a person succumbed to the addiction. Crack houses in the rural south were nothing more than shacks that were owned or rented by the addicted person that allowed drug deals to be made. It was generally a common meeting ground for those who were addicted to the use of or sell of the drug.

Theft and robbery reached unusual heights. Addicted people or "crack heads" spared no one in an attempt to obtain the drug.

Normally, it was nothing personal but the feeling was something that must be chased at all costs by the "crack head".

Subsequently, by the end of the nineties, the age of high school fraternal orders slowly began to slip into non existence within the rural south. Fraternity ideology was in direct conflict with the ideology of gangs. In previous years, it was unheard of for young African Americans who lived in the rural south to even consider participating in a gang. They would flee from the idea of daring to associate themselves with such an activity or involvement and fought to keep that type of thinking out of the confines of their existence. By the mid to late nineties, however, young African Americans living within the rural south embraced the ideology of gangs with open arms leaving the fraternal system to struggle and possibly die.

Countless African American young men were arrested and sent to prison with stiffer penalties sometimes than murdering another human as a consequence for selling a drug that they never had the means to grow and transport into the country. Tragically, however, they are continuously replaced by others who feel that they will one day become "The Man."

HIV/AIDS also began to ravish the African American rural south as quickly and as easily as crack had. Safe sex was a hilarious idea to the minds of African American rural southerners. It was a strong belief that the disease was only a white homosexual man's disease, hence, it could never reach the confines of the "back woods" or the stoic little communities that did nothing but work, go to church, shop, eat, and have sex. Furthermore, there were so few gay men living in the rural south that it could not possibly reach those parts of the nation.

Ha!

HIV/AIDS has a mind of its own and it, like drugs, will defend itself at all costs!

HIV/AIDS did reach the African American rural south and soon became an epidemic among men, women, and children.

When it seemed that the African American rural south had received double destruction with crack and AIDS on the rampage within the community, it was not possibly enough to destroy the sanctity and nostalgia of the area. This was not enough for the new youth of the African American rural south.

Violence began to engulf much of the entire rural south.

It was absolutely nothing for young people to loose their lives in a frivolous argument. People no longer fought with fists, sticks, and knives. This had all been replaced with guns and more guns and more guns. Guns permanently settled conflicts!

Not all things suffered as a result of the changing rural south. The court system, the prisons, the pharmaceutical companies, health care industry, and the mortuaries have prospered greatly during this transformation.

Frederick's words *I want to die young and beautiful* began to haunt Melvin. The tragedy of the horrific crime committed against Frederick just would not leave Melvin's mind.

Evening began to enter on the horizon of Fairhaven.

Melvin began to become angry because night time approached. He could not understand why he had become so angry at such a natural part of life.

Yet, he was.

In order to calm his nerves, he walked into his study, turned his computer on, and pulled up his journal on the monitor. Seldom did he write poetry yet he was suddenly compelled. He began to write:

You, Night, stretch forth

your hand

covering the day

kike a mother

who wraps her child

in a blanket.

Can you protect,

Oh, Night,
the imagination
from itself?

Imagination,
how vivid
your tales may be!
You take us
to another land
where there are
no hurts,
no troubles,
no trials!
You laugh
only to remind us
there is also
no joy
no happiness
no peace
no calm –
just an abyss
of false dreams
and desires!

You, Imagination,
love to visit,
although not invited,
the poor in distress,

who knows no
Hope!
You visit
the sick in
weary affliction
who prays
for the benevolence of
Mercy!

You, Imagination,
visit the halls
of royalty!
Your advice, Imagination,
has caused wars
and rumors of wars.
Smugly you smile
as if
you know not how
your twisted tongue
confounds the minds
of mortal men.
Your power is strong –
only if allowed!
Your sister, Hope,
has a stronger hold
on humanity.
Did you not know?

Beloved, Hope,

how inspiring
you can be
when Despair lurks
at every door
of Opportunity.
What a refreshing enchantment,
Hope, knowing
you are present!
You, Hope,
calm fears
in the time of trouble.
You add
beauty
charm
poise
elegance
and eloquence
to a desolate moment
in the weary lives
of mere callous
mortal men.

Grace and Mercy,
you dashing twins,
that plea the cause
of the oppressed.
How gallant
you are

in action!
Will you plead
the Great Case
of the lost souls
of Life's war?

Night, oh Night,
what friends
you have,
indeed!
Colleagues both,
good and bad,
constantly close
in fellowship!

Innumerable thoughts raced through Melvin's mind as he dressed for Frederick's wake. The police seemed to drag their feet in attempting to catch Frederick's murderer. The investigation was a complete farce. First, the police questioned Bradley because he was the last person actually seen with Frederick. Bradley was quite insulted because he knew that he had gone home immediately after he dropped Frederick off. The police was prepared to close the case and label it suicide until The Rev, Grimlock, and Light bulb spoke directly to the mayor and threatened an N.A.A.C.P. rally against the police force. When this tactic seemed as if it would not work, The Rev, Grimlock, and Light Bulb threatened to withdraw political support from the mayor. At this, a new detective was placed on the case.

A major argument had occurred within the Omega Complex between the Alumni Council. Howard requested that Frederick's wake be held at the Omega Complex being he had served as a Senator from Newbern when he was in high school and being that he faithfully paid his Alumni Council dues although he had become an inactive member.

"We are not going to glorify some fag who died a bad death," one of the new member's of the Council commented during a special called meeting for the purpose of voting on the subject matter.

A hush fell across the room.

Indeed there was always quiet before the storm.

All eyes drifted toward Howard.

"I tell you what," Bradley said. "You al can vote however you want to but just let the vote be "no!" If that happens, I will personally do everything in my power to see to it that every gay or bi-sexual or even gay friendly Alumni member protest and stop paying dues. Then we will see just how much it really matters."

"You all didn't worry about Frederick's sexual orientation when you all accepted his membership dues," Desmond said. "Nor did you have a problem with his sexual orientation when he made a contribution to the annual scholarship fund. You all know that he really couldn't afford it but he always gave over a hundred dollars to that event and y'all know it!"

A slight murmur could be heard across the room.

"First of all," The Rev said. "We, as an organization, must remember that regardless of his sexual orientation, he is still our brother. When any candidate pledges and becomes a member, he is a brother and is entitled to all rights and privileges of any other member. What does the Constitution say about our obligations to deceased members?"

The Rev had recently been elected Moderator of the Alumni Council. After his graduation, he left Dyersburg in pursuit of his bachelor's degree at Tennessee State University in Nashville, Tennessee. After his graduation, he returned to the area to establish his accounting firm that became a success. Because he, like all other Alumni of Omega Phi Theta, had an endearing place within his heart for the fading organization, he was elected Moderator of the Alumni Council. Once again, he had replaced Light Bulb who also remained in Dyersburg and had become the vice-president of a local shipping firm.

"The Constitution states in Amendment 30.1," the Executive Secretary began to read. "Any member of this organization who has served a term in the congressional Order between the years of 1985 – 1995 and dies shall be entitled full use of The Bennie L. Jackson, II Congressional Hall whereas his body shall lie in state. If requested by his family or brothers, he may also be funeralized in the aforementioned hall."

"What are other obligations to past and present members of the Alumni Association upon death?" the Rev asked.

"Amendment 30.2 reads," The Executive Secretary read. "The Dean of historical Archives' Office shall be responsible issuing a Resolution from the Omega Phi theta Fraternity that shall be read at the funeral. This office shall also purchase a floral spray on behalf of the organization. The spray shall be sent to the funeral home where the body is located. The spray shall not exceed a cost of $75. Last, this office shall be responsible for sending a sympathy card on behalf of the fraternity to the family."

"Well," The Rev said." May I get a motion to follow procedures of the Constitution. We do still follow the Constitution?"

"So moved," Desmond called.

"Second," another person yelled.

"The wake of Frederick Perry will be held here at the Omega Complex!" the Rev stated firmly. "The family can choose the Bennie L. Jackson, II, Congressional Hall or the Terry Lee White Ball Room, whichever is most convenient. I expect each officer and member of this organization to give the Perry Family and friends total and complete respect during the services!"

"What if one of those fags makes a pass at one of us?" one of the opponents of Bradley commented.

"Just say *No*," The Rev said. "If there is no more pertinent business, may I have a motion to adjourn this meeting?"

"So moved," Melvin said quickly.

Chapter Fourteen
I'm Working On My Building

I'm working on my building!
It's a sure foundation!
I'm holding up the Bloodstained
Banner for my Lord.
Just as soon as I get through
Working on my building
I'm going up to Heaven
To get my reward!

Melvin entered the Omega Complex at fifteen minutes after seven on the night of Frederick's wake. The voices of The Clark Sisters echoed through the foyer as Melvin walked through and exchanged pleasantries with various people who came to pay their respects to the deceased. He walked to the doors of the Terry L. White Ball Room and signed his name on the last available page of the register that sat atop a stand that had been provided by The James Funeral Home. Melvin noticed how the register had begun to bulge with sympathy cards. He became immediately frustrated.

"Excuse me," he whispered to an usher who stood nearby. "Someone needs to get these cards and put them in a separate place so this book won't bulge so."

"We just removed one stack," a familiar voice said. The voice was immediately behind him. Melvin looked up into the eyes of The Rev who towered over him.

"As quickly as we remove one stack, another one builds up," The Rev said. "Rest assured, though, it is under control!"

"Thanks," Melvin smiled slightly as he turned away from The Rev to look inside of the Hall where Frederick's corpse lay. Large floral sprays and potted plants encompassed the entire room. The casket appeared engulfed in a bed of lilies while the sprays loomed high into the air. Because there were so many, Melvin felt as if the flowers made Frederick's casket look smaller than it actually was.

Lethargy began to settle over Melvin.

He quickly surveyed the room for the presence of Bradley, Desmond, Douglas, Howard, or even Xavier.

He did not see any of them.

He knew that he could not view Frederick's body alone without the aid of his friends. He was definitely not into causing a scene yet he knew that to see Frederick lying in a casket now would cause his emotions to stir wildly.

The Rev, who had not left his side, sensed Melvin's apprehension.

"You don't have to do this now," The Rev said.

Melvin was comforted at The Rev's sincere gesture.

"I need to take a walk," Melvin confessed. "Then I'll come back!"

"Would you like to go to my office?" The Rev suggested. "After I was elected moderator of the alumni, I had the room renovated. Light bulb kept things a little too basic for my taste."

"I certainly could use the change of scenery and a breath of fresh air," Melvin said. "Plus, I'd love to see what you've done with it too. I haven't been to any meetings in a while, so, I didn't even know you had renovated it."

Melvin and The Rev walked to The Rev's newly renovated office briefly speaking to various mourners who filled the Omega Complex. As they walked, Melvin noted that The Rev was always there for him whenever he needed him the most.

The Rev's office was fabulously renovated in comparison to the previous office of Light Bulb when he held the office of Moderator. As The Rev had noted, Light Bulb's office had been plain bearing only a desk, cabinets, and a few photographs. The Rev's renovation made the office seem inviting and comfortable. The huge mahogany desk that sat in the center of the room was polished to perfection. Two Queen Anne chairs sat at the ends of the front of the desk. Behind the desk, The Rev enjoyed a huge swivel leather chair. On the wall hung The Rev's degrees, awards, and photos taken while in the fraternity. Silk plants were strategically placed about the room.

The Rev sat down in his chair as they entered the office while Melvin sat in a Queen Anne Chair facing him.

"This is nice," Melvin commented as he viewed the luxury of the room.

"I hope so," The Rev laughed. "I actually renovated my office at work and just sent this stuff over here from my old office. You know that no one wants to take care of the moderator since I was elected, you all used to keep Light Bulb spoiled."

"These are difficult times," Melvin chuckled.

Melvin was happy to be in The Rev's presence after so many years had gone by. The Rev had managed to lift his spirits which only made Melvin feel a sweet serenity and security while in his presence. The Rev and Melvin talked for over an hour simply reminiscing over the past and how glorious it all seemed then. The longer the two of them talked, however, the more old feelings began to rise in Melvin for The Rev.

At certain moments during the conversation, Melvin would simply watch The Rev. He really didn't hear any words come forth from The Rev's mouth yet there was a certain comfort in watching The Rev as his face seemed to illuminate whenever he talked about the past.

Melvin could not purge himself of the old feelings. Once again, his hero from the past sat in front of him

The Rev, in Melvin's opinion, was ageless and looked as handsome as he had well over ten years prior when they first met. The Jherri curl had been replaced with a low cut fade. The mustache was still trimmed to an almost hairline just above his lips. His lips were still full. He wore eye glasses now that made him look even more distinguished.

"What are you staring at," The Rev asked. "I don't have anything on my face do I?"

"No," Melvin replied. "I was just thinking about how you really have not changed a bit in almost ten years. You still look as handsome as you did in high school."

"Well, thank you," The Rev blushed. "You don't look bad yourself, as a matter of fact, you are still as cute as you were back in high school too."

Melvin's heart leaped.

The Rev had just paid him a compliment for the first time ever!

"You know," Melvin honestly and openly confessed. "I had a crush on you back in the day."

"Sometimes I could tell." The Rev said. "It looks like you've gotten over that infatuation now."

"Sometimes," Melvin laughed. "I often wonder what life could have been like if we had become lovers?"

"Back then," The Rev confessed. "I wasn't ready for all of that! I had to grow into my sexuality and the journey has been a journey indeed. But I am comfortable with whom I am and that is really all that matters."

"What about now?" Melvin asked.

"I'd love to," The Rev said. "But I really can't offer you anything except friendship right now."

Melvin's heart leaped again. He didn't know exactly where this was leading yet he had to stick around to understand exactly where The Rev was coming from.

"So," Melvin asked. "You would date me if the opportunity presented itself?"

"I certainly would," The rev replied.

Again, Melvin's heart leaped.

He almost could not believe that he had heard The Rev correctly.

"What's stopping you now?" Melvin asked. "Hopefully, not this fraternity!"

"Please," The Rev laughed. "This fraternity has nothing to do with my personal life."

The Rev stood up and walked around and sat in a Queen Anne chair beside Melvin. He grabbed both of Melvin's hands and held them within his. Melvin thanked God that the door had been closed upon them entering the room.

"Melvin," The Rev continued. "You are an awfully attractive man! Even right now you still have the power to make my nature rise but you deserve better than what I can offer you right now. The only thing that I could offer you right now would be sex and still it would be unfair to you."

"Why is that?" Melvin asked.

"I have a partner," The Rev said. "I wouldn't consider cheating on him because I do practice monogamy. We've been together now for almost two years and I am madly in love with him."

"I appreciate your honesty," Melvin said as he thought about everything that The Rev had said.

"He finally admitted that he is gay," Melvin thought. *"Lord, what is the world coming to? He also said that he has a man that he is in love with… Damn!"*

The Rev looked at his watch and realized that it was twenty minutes until nine.

"I think was had better get back out there," The Rev said. "It is almost time for the wake to be over and I have to conduct the Omega-Omega-Omega Services over the body. Are you ok or is there anything else that you would like to talk about?"

"Yes," Melvin said. "There is!"

"Let's hear it," The Rev said.

"How much money is the fraternity going to contribute to Frederick's funeral?" Melvin asked. "You know that he didn't have insurance and his family disowned him years ago."

"What?" The Rev asked in horror.

"You don't see his parents or his family members here tonight," Melvin stated. "You will not see them tomorrow at the funeral either. The only family that he had was the few fraternity members that he hung out with."

"Lord, have mercy," The Rev said. "How much money do you need and who do I need to send the check to?"

"Well, I talked my dad into doing a lot of it for free," Melvin said. "But as a business man, he wants some type of compensation for all of this."

"I noticed how expensive everything looks," The Rev commented. "Did you pick out all of this? How much did all of this cost?"

"Actually, Bradley and Desmond insisted that we spend $2500 on the casket and another $1000 on the vault," Melvin explained. "Dad refuses to give up his merchandise without us paying him something. So, I just asked him for the bill and he sent me a bill for over $8500."

"Well," The Rev asked. "How much have you guys raised between you all?'

"Well, Desmond gave $1000, Bradley gave $1500 Howard gave $1000, Douglas gave $500, William gave $500 and Xavier gave $1000," Melvin said. "I put in $1500 and that only totals $7,000. We are still $1500 shy of our goal."

The Rev stood up and walked back to his desk. He opened a drawer and pulled out a checkbook.

The Rev wrote a check out and placed it in Melvin's hand.

Melvin looked down at it and noticed that it was from The Rev's personal checks and not the fraternity's.

It was a check for $2000.

"What's the other five hundred dollars for?" Melvin asked as tears began to sting his eyes.

"He needs a headstone," The Rev said.

"Thanks," Melvin said, stood up, and hugged The Rev tightly.

He could not resist.

Melvin decided against going back into the ballroom where Frederick's corpse lay. Surprisingly, throughout the entire process of preparing for Frederick's funeral, he had not seen Frederick in the casket yet. He, Bradley, Desmond, Douglas, Howard, and Xavier had met at his father's funeral home and bargained for hours with Melvin's father. Clarence sympathized with their views but he was still a business man. He could not allow his merchandise to leave the funeral home without being paid for and he didn't care who it was. Together, the group agreed to Clarence's terms and then picked out the casket and clothing that Frederick would be buried in. When they had completed making all of the necessary arrangements, they all went their separate ways in order to raise the money that would have been needed to "properly" bury their friend.

After hugging The Rev, Melvin went home and dismissed anything associated with a funeral. He just wanted to relax his mind and soul knowing that the next day; he would have to face seeing his friend in a coffin. But tonight was not the night!

Chapter Fifteen

I'll Fly Away

Some glad morning when this life is over
I'll fly away!
To a home on God's celestial shore!
I'll fly away!
I'll fly away, oh glory!
I'll fly away!
When I die hallelujah by and by
I'll fly away!

Mt. Carmel Baptist Church of Fairhaven, Tennessee was not prepared for the funeral services of Frederick Perry. Although Mt. Carmel had a relatively large edifice and was able to seat 550 people, seats were placed in the aisles after the balcony quickly filled with mourners and on-lookers of the deceased. Because Rev. William Barnes actually knew Frederick, Melvin and Bradley had asked him to give the eulogy while Rev. Garrison, the pastor of Mt. Carmel, was asked to officiate the services. Howard's community choir was scheduled to furnish the music. When news traveled into the community that Frederick's family refused to attend the funeral, the members of the Omega Phi Theta Fraternity Alumni Association and Frederick's closest friends filled the reserved section of the pews normally reserved for family.

Melvin, Bradley, Desmond, Douglas, and Xavier led the procession into the church while Howard played soft music. Melvin sat on the front pew beside a very distraught Bradley. Desmond sat next to Bradley and Douglas sat on his right. Xavier sat on the corner pew to Melvin's left.

Melvin was terribly sad at the beginning of the services until Howard's choir stood up and began to sing. The mood of the entire services changed from somber and sad to joyous and "churchy."

The choir sang three songs back to back at the beginning of the services that were very upbeat. Melvin knew that traditionally he was trained to be somber and reverent at the burial of the dead at Mt. Carmel yet he could not help himself. He, like many of the other people who attended the services, began to clap, sway, and even sing as the choir bellowed out:

"Long As I Got King Jesus, I Don't Need Nobody Else"

"I'm On My Way to Heaven to Meet the King"

and

"He'll Welcome Me Home"

Melvin could do nothing but smile when he thought about how "untraditional" the entire occasion had become. The Scriptures and prayer delivered by the various ministers were not the normal Scriptures that Melvin ad experienced at former funerals yet they somehow seemed appropriate. The ministers who read them and the minister who prayed almost seemed as if they were preaching rather than reading a Scripture or delivering a prayer.

The choir stood up at the close of the prayer and sang:

"God Is A Right Now God"

Melvin knew that the occasion had definitely turned into a "Home Going Celebration" rather than the funeral and mourning of a man who had been murdered.

When the choir finished their selection and the audience had settled slightly, The Rev walked to the side podium and read resolutions from the Omega Phi Theta Fraternity. When he finished, Mrs. Geneva Porter, Mt. Carmel's Church clerk, read resolutions from Mt. Carmel and various other churches.

For a moment, Melvin felt that the resolutions that Mrs. Porter read did not describe the life of the Frederick that he had known at all. Yet people were merely trying to be nice.

Melvin could not contain his grief when Xavier went to the podium.

"Frederick loved good singing," Xavier said. "He was probably one of my greatest fans! I remember that we were here in this very church a few years back when Frederick received the Lord Jesus Christ in his life! The choir sang *I'm Looking For A Miracle* on that night. Mt. Carmel went forth and yet Frederick did not move out of his seat. Someone requested that I sing a song and I decided to sing this song. My heart overflowed with joy when Frederick got up out of his seat and accepted Christ! I thank God that through the persuasion of my voice, he was saved!"

Howard began to churn out a churchy/blues introduction on the organ that made the listener know that a familiar traditional gospel song was about to be sung.

The crowd began to clap in beat of the music before Xavier began his song, although Xavier began to hum.

Xavier threw his head back and began to bellow out

"One of these mornings…
Soon one morning….
I'm gonna lay down my cross and get me a crown"

Tears streamed down Melvin's face as Xavier sang.

"Late one evening
Late in the evening
Late in the evening, child
I'm going home to live on High!"

"Frederick, Frederick, Frederick," Desmond cried out as he hunched over in his seat.

"I'm going outside seeing in Beulah…
March all around God's altar
I'm gonna fly and never falter
I'm gonna live, Lord, forever!

"You better sang, boy," someone in the audience yelled.

As Xavier's voice rose, Howard matched him on the organ.

"Oh, will you be there, early in the morning?
Will you be there somewhere 'round God's altar?
Will you be there, oh when the Angels shall call the roll?'

People began to stand up.

Screams could be heard throughout the sanctuary.

Tears were constant in Melvin's eyes and yet he could not move.

Bradley wiped tears but sat stoically.

"Oh, Frederick!" Desmond wailed as Douglas held him tightly.

It will be always
Always "Howdy, Howdy!"
And
Never
Never
Never
It will never be "Good bye!"

The crowd first gave a thunderous applause as Howard continued to play. The organ literally sounded as if it were singing the words that Xavier had. Then, his music changed.

Xavier began to sing as Howard's music changed:

"There are just a few more weary days and then
I, oh yes I will, I'm gonna fly away!
To a land where joy, joy it shall never end
Oh, I, oh yes, I
I'm gonna fly away!

The ministers on the roster could not take it.

They stood up and joined Xavier in singing the chorus.

I'll fly away, oh glory!
I'll fly away!
When I die hallelujah by and by
I'll fly away!

The sounds of muffled crying and sniffling could be heard throughout the sanctuary when Xavier took his seat.

William stood up, waited for the congregation to settle down and then proceeded to give the eulogy.

"This is a very hard task before me today," William began. *"Nevertheless, I will begin by saying that Frederick is in the hands of a just God! I'm so glad that we don't have a Heaven or a hell to put him in. The most important thing, however, is that we have a personal relationship with our Maker..."*

"Say that," an elderly woman yelled.

Melvin tuned William completely out. He could not bear listening to another word! He felt that he could scream at the top of his voice. His emotions of grief perplexed him. He was angry at the least of things and within second of his anger he would became extremely happy. He would think of some phrase that Frederick would have said and somehow his grief would transform into happiness. When he felt sad, a song would enter his mind that would lift his spirits. When he felt happy, another song would enter his mind that made him want to cry. When he desired the strength to cry, not ears would fall from his face. When he desired the strength to keep a straight face, tears would fall without warning.

Throughout William's eulogy, Melvin tried hard to get his emotions under control. Occasionally, Bradley would sniffle. Desmond cried out, so it seemed, at every word that William said.

Melvin felt that he could no longer be of any assistance to his friends until he could get his own emotions under control. He needed some type of consolation and yet he could find it nowhere.

William ended his eulogy/sermon and the choir stood and sang *Hold On, Help Is On The Way!*

Two attendants from James Funeral home stood like statues at the head and foot of Frederick's casket. A third attendant came and began to open the casket. Howard began to play softly.

"My Christian friends," one of the attendants began in his normal monotonous litany. "We thank you for attending today's home Going Celebration of the late Brother Frederick Perry. We shall now participate in the last glimpse before Glory! We ask that you please follow the direction of the attendants, whereas, all confusion will be completely alleviated. We ask that the ministers begin, followed by those of you who are seated in the aisles, followed by the choir."

Soon, people from every walk of life began to file past Frederick's casket to get a "final glimpse" of him

Melvin hated this tradition with every fiber of his existence.

He could not see the point in people gawking at you while you were in your casket before you were buried.

The choir began to sing *It's An Uphill journey To Glory!*

Soon, the time came for Melvin to be escorted to the casket.

His breath became short.

His legs became weak.

The closer that he walked towards his friend in this box, the worse things became for him.

Tears streamed down his face in great waves.

He had avoided this moment. He had not seen Frederick since he had looked upon him in his apartment. He had every opportunity to view Frederick's body prior to this point; after all, his father's funeral home was in charge of the arrangements. He could have spent hours with Frederick's embalmed body is he had desired. Now, at his weakest moment with his emotions in complete conflict, he looked into the casket of his friend.

Frederick truly did look asleep.

He looked better than he ever had.

Melvin's legs no longer supported him.

He became hot, dizzy, confused...

Everything went **black.**

When Melvin awoke, his mother was dabbing his forehead with water.

"What happened?" Melvin asked.

"You fainted, baby," Etta said.

Melvin attempted to rise from the sofa that he was lying on.

"Just be still for a little while longer," Etta said as she gently pushed him backward onto the sofa. "You need to collect your faculties!"

Melvin tried desperately to figure out where he was.

The room was unfamiliar to him and yet he recognized it.

"Where am I, Momma?" he asked.

"We are in the Pastor's Study," Etta said. "It was the only place your fraternity brothers could carry you quickly."

"I didn't know you were coming today," Melvin said.

"Baby, you are my son and I love you no matter what," Etta said. "If ever you needed your momma, you needed me today and right now!"

"Thanks, Momma," Melvin said as he hugged his mother's tiny frame.

Melvin began to rise from his position of lying down.

Etta did not prevent him on this attempt as she had previously.

"Momma," Melvin said as tears began to well in his eyes. "I don't want to die like that!"

"You won't, baby," Etta said as she hugged him and began to rock him back and forth in the same manner she had when he was a small boy. "Frederick was just too trusting! You are far more cautious like your Uncle Claiborne."

Melvin tried to understand the parallelism.

"Momma," Melvin said softly.

"Yes, baby," she answered him.

"Did you know that I am gay?" he asked earnestly.

"I carried you for nine months, Melvin," she said as she drew him closer to her. "I've known about it for years, baby. It changes nothing. I love you and you are still my child!"

Melvin looked into his mother's eyes and noticed the tears that streamed down her face.

"I don't want to hurt you, Momma," Melvin said as tears began to roll down his own face. "Please, don't cry!"

"You haven't hurt me, child," she said as she wiped tears away with a white handkerchief that had been trimmed in lace. "I just can't imagine losing any of my children but to lose a child and not attend the funeral services…"

"Well, Momma," Melvin said. "It's like you always said: *You reap what you sow!* Frederick's mother has to reap this for the remainder of her life!"

"What a waste," Etta said as she released Melvin and began to gain her composure. She pulled a compact out of her purse which sat nearby and looked into it as she lightly dusted her face with a powder puff.

Melvin felt as if he were the luckiest man on earth!

Although this was one of his weakest moments in life, he had managed to gain the strength to "come out" to his mother. Most important, however, she had accepted him with tender and loving arms.

Etta looked through the window at Bradley, Douglas, Desmond, Howard and Xavier. They were sadly walking to the burial site where Frederick would soon be laid to rest. Fortunately, Frederick's grandmother had been a member and after Frederick had joined the church, the cost of the plot was free for him to be buried in the Mt. Carmel Cemetery.

"Son," Etta said.

"Yes, Momma?" Melvin replied.

"You need to go and be with your friends," she advised. "They are hurting just as badly as you are right now. They need you and you need them. If you guys ever realized that there is strength in numbers you would never have to worry about anything like this happening again."

"We thought we had just that, Momma," Melvin said.

"Well," Etta commented. "You can't stop now!"

Melvin looked out of the window at his friends.

"Frederick once said that he wanted the children to just get together," Melvin grinned slightly.

"Why not begin now," she said softly.

The End

This is an absolutely adorable tale of an African-American teen brat-pack, their trials, dreams, disappointments, self-realizations and successes. Beginning with their middle school friendship, Smith manages to give each character a distinct personality and unquestionable maturity level, while still retaining the naivety needed to make for believable characters. The meticulously placed humor will make you laugh aloud and the dramatic reality of its lowest moments will bring you to tears. This behind the scenes peek into the private lives of teens in the rural south is both refreshing and eye opening. This is one NOT to miss...

~Caesar Brunswick~

Smith captured the essence of the rural south in a single novel. "When The Children Get Together" keeps the reader flipping pages as the characters come to life with each page. Smith proves to be one of the greatest writers of this particular genre that has come on the scene. If one has not read or obtained a copy of this novel, you have missed one of the greatest opportunities of a life time.

~ Amazon.com Reader ~